BOOKS BY LEON HALE

Turn South at the Second Bridge (1965)
Bonney's Place (1972)
Addison (1979)
A Smile From Katie Hattan (1982)
Easy Going (1983)
One Man's Christmas (1984)

Paper Hero

PAPER HERO

Leon Hale

Shearer Publishing/Fredericksburg, Texas

Library of Congress Cataloging-in-Publication Data

Hale, Leon, 1921-
Paper hero.
1. Hale, Leon—Biography—Youth. 2. Authors, American—20th
Century—Biography. I. Title.
PS3558.A357Z47   1986   813'.54 B   86-13011
ISBN 0-940672-36-7

Manufactured in the United States of America
First Edition

Cover illustration by Lee Ethel

Shearer Publishing
406 Post Oak Road
Fredericksburg, Texas 78624

Contents

In celebration of the lives of
LEONA MAY OXFORD HALE
and
FRED D. HALE

Paper Hero

The Fire

THE WINTER *of 1927, when I was six years old, I became a hero for the first time. I saved the lives of my
entire family, with the exception of my father. I saved my mother
and my two sisters and a white Persian cat. My father was out in
the back yard milking the cow or I would have saved him as well.
Just before dawn I began to smell smoke and saw right away that
the house was burning. I sprang out of bed and rescued my sisters.
They were both older than I was but I rescued them anyhow. I
woke them and herded them, all sleepy and confused, into the
yard. I went back into the flaming house and rescued my mother
who was cooking oatmeal in the kitchen, as she did every morning for half a century. Then I returned and got the cat. All of us
huddled in the yard and watched the house burn. It was wonderful. People came to watch with us. People we didn't even know.
They asked us personal questions that weren't any of their business and we answered them eagerly. The fire truck came and
brought real firemen who clodded through our house and shouted
and shot water all around, and a woman next door cooked us a
strange breakfast without oatmeal. I had never done a thing that
made me feel half as fine. Up to the time of the fire I had not been
able to see that my life was of any value. But now I recognized
that it was my purpose to be heroic now and then.*

The fire had started from the coal-burning stove. This was when we lived in the little West Texas town of Stamford. Not much wood was available around there and many families heated their houses with coal. If our stove was overloaded with coal, the stovepipe going up through the roof would get red-hot and the ceiling would catch fire, and the roof.

The person who built the fire too hot was my father. He had a tendency to overdo things that way. He would even overdo a thing like putting on his shoes. If he put on a shoe at five o'clock in the morning when everybody else was asleep, and if he needed to stomp his foot a little to make the shoe finish going on, he would stomp hard enough to kill a snake. The stomp would shake the house. It would rattle dishes in the kitchen safe.

Also he slammed doors, and kicked small objects when he wanted them moved. Leaving for work, he started his car in this same thunderous manner. As quick as he got the engine going he would jam the gas pedal to the floorboard and keep it there a long while and the engine would scream in torment. Even before I knew about such things as pistons and connecting rods, I imagined that if he didn't take his big foot off the accelerator soon, pieces of hot metal would come ripping through the hood and shower the premises.

When he took a bath, everybody in the house knew it because he made these spectacular splashing and sloshing noises. It is my belief that he somehow arranged his six-foot person into a mass that fit exactly into a little claw-footed bathtub, so that no arms or legs were left sticking out. Then he rolled violently in the water, over and over many times. I don't see how he could have produced such a disturbance any other way. I was never able to face him and ask what his system was but I did ask my mother. She shook her head slowly and put on her most solemn face.

"I don't know," she answered. "I've always wondered."

Many years later, when I had grown up and left home and come back for a visit, I heard him in the bathroom making his splashing sounds the same as ever and I asked my mother again. Had she ever found out how he did it?

"No, but one of these days I'm going to slip in there and spy on him and see."

They had then been married more than forty years. So you see my father was not an easy person to talk to regarding private matters. But I loved him fiercely, and I was sorry I didn't get to save him from the fire along with the others.

The winter the house burned, he was working in a dry goods store. It would be called a clothing store now, I guess, or a department store. He opened that store six mornings a week at seven o'clock, so his time of getting out of bed was around five. I would lie still and listen to his various noises.

First the stomping, to get his shoes on. Then the washing of his face, which gave off a combination of startling growls and blubbers and hoots. Sometimes he gargled. His gargling was magnificent. Nobody would be left asleep in the house if he gargled.

Next he built the fire too hot in the stove. When he got it going he would clank the poker a few times against the stove leg. Then he would raise the coal shovel and drop it into the scuttle from an altitude of about four feet, I suppose so that it would make a satisfactory amount of noise. He would go next to the back porch, rattle the milk bucket, slam the door, stomp down the back steps and out to the cow lot.

Eccentricities like these were never talked about in our house. We did not complain about them, or make jokes about them. So it didn't much bother me that nothing was said at home about my heroics in connection with that fire. I supposed I had done no more than was expected of me, and it didn't need discussing. If my sisters had a homework assignment to diagram twenty-six sentences, and they diagrammed them every one exactly right, this was not celebrated at home. They were *expected* to diagram sentences perfectly, and I have to say that both those girls did what was expected of them, at diagramming sentences or anything else, and to this day you

cannot devise a sentence, including this one, sufficiently awkward or convoluted that they can't diagram it in a split minute
with one hand tied behind their backs.

The first time my role in that fire was spoken of in our
house, I was up in school to the place where they made us
write what we called themes. I wrote one about the fire and
got a passing grade. It was in fact an excellent mark, consid-
ering that I hadn't had a formal introduction to the art of
spelling.

In that theme I told the story of the fire just about the same
as I have told it to you in the preceding pages. I took the paper
home, since the grade on it was passing, and showed it at the
supper table. I was puzzled by the reaction.

"The house didn't burn to the ground," my sisters said,
reading the theme. "The fire was all in the attic and the firemen put it out up there. It never did get to the kitchen."

That was a reference to my account of how I placed a damp
cup towel over the face of my mother and led her out of the
flaming kitchen into the cold night, where her precious lungs
could breathe in pure air.

"This is all wrong," they said. They were disappointed
in me. They loved me and wanted me to be perfect, just as
they were when they diagrammed sentences and memorized
poems. "You didn't rescue Mama. She was the one who called
the fire department. You didn't rescue us, either. Mama came
and got us and when we went to wake you up, you had gone
to the bathroom and we had to wait for you to get through.

"And you say here that you rescued Puff [the cat] off the
roof. She wasn't on the roof. She was sleeping on our bed and
we carried her out. And what's this about a smoking nightshirt? You never had a nightshirt in your life. You've always
slept in your underwear."

A Sears-Roebuck catalog is where I got the smoking nightshirt. It had a section for something called "nightclothes" for
men and boys. One page showed pictures of good-looking
muscley boys in nightshirts. I had never owned a nightshirt,
just as my sisters said, but I imagined that wearing one would
make me look like those model-boys in the catalog. So I put

one on, in my account of the fire, and climbed up the lattice-work and rescued the terrified cat and descended with smoke coming out of my nightshirt.

I was able to see that my sisters' attitude toward my heroics during that fire was very likely the product of jealousy. They were girls, don't forget. Therefore they were not able to climb onto roofs and save cats. I understood it wasn't their fault. It was simply that heroics was for boys, and diagramming sentences was for girls.

Another factor is that, for some reason not clear to me, these sisters are not able to recall events and circumstances in the detail that I can.

For instance, they can't remember that the red rooster swallowed our mother's wedding ring when we were living in Stephenville, the town where I originated. I had been originated only four years when the rooster swallowed the ring. Nevertheless, I can see the ring on a rock in our back yard. I can see the rooster eyeing it. Then pecking at it, twice, in an experimental way. Then gobbling it down. He was a Rhode Island Red rooster.

My sister Maifred says now that the rooster swallowed a ring, all right, but it wasn't our mother's wedding band. She says the ring was hers, a tiny Sunday School ring she had been awarded at the First Methodist Church. She got the ring for memorizing the names of the books of the Bible. She says she had taken the ring off while she was feeding the chickens and put it down on a rock and the rooster got it. She says our mother would never have taken her wedding band off and put it down on a rock.

That same sister insists that the rooster wasn't killed to re-trieve the ring. I say he was. Because my father came home at noon from the store and I can see him running after that old red bird. My father wore a white shirt and a blue tie and gray pants and a pretty yellow summer straw hat with a black band. I believe that was the first time I'd ever seen a grown man running full-out that way. And he was my own father, dressed for work, and the sight impressed me and so I know it's a valid recollection.

Seeing him catch the rooster and wring its neck is not as clear a memory as it might be but it's clear enough to suit me, if not my sisters. I expect you'll agree it's extraordinary that a girl bright enough to memorize the books of the Bible, from Genesis to Revelations, can't recall that she saw a large Rhode Island Red rooster eat her own mother's wedding ring.

Consider the matter of the sleepwalk. My sister Maifred once performed a spectacular sleepwalk when she was a young girl. This was the most important thing that had happened in our family up until the fire. She went out of the house in the middle of the night, walked all the way to town, in the rain, and got halfway around the Erath County Courthouse Square before our father caught her and woke her up in front of Higginbotham's Dry Goods Store.

This sister maintains today that she did no such thing. She says she walked out the back door in her sleep, yes, and she will also grant me that it was raining. But she says our father caught up to her not ten steps out the door and brought her back in.

How could this be true? If it is, why would I be able to see her walking in her nightgown past Higginbotham's on the west side of the courthouse square?

My other sister, Ima Ruthie, has very little better recollection, if any, of these events. She doesn't even remember the Booger Man that stayed in the garage of the Homeyers who lived next door to us in Stephenville. How anybody could forget such a creature is past my understanding. The eyes of the thing were the size of pie plates. It was the reason I would never go past the Homeyers' garage except in a dead run. Why do you suppose she thought I was running that way all the time?

She also refuses to remember playing the piano by ear when she was four years old. But I was a witness to that. I saw her standing flat-footed at the piano, eyes level with the keyboard, and reaching up and playing Brahms' "Lullaby." This was when she didn't know a note of music. She didn't know middle C from a clap of thunder. All the same, she could play

Brahms, and "Yankee Doodle," and "Old Black Joe," and now she can't remember it. For fifty years I have been telling people that my sister could play Brahms by ear when she was four and I know it must be true or else I wouldn't have gone around talking about it so much.

In the pages to follow, I intend to record many other events that shaped our lives in those curious years when we were all under the same roof. We don't always agree on the details of those events. But that doesn't mean I am telling things wrong. I am telling everything just the way it needs to be told.

The Car

L ATE IN 1945, I was rich for a while. I had been in the Army three years and one of those years I spent in Europe. Every month I sent my mother $200 from Italy to put in the bank for me. When I came home in November of '45 I had $2,400 waiting for me. My mother was proud of that money. Nobody in our family had ever had that much in the bank.

"What are you going to do with it?" she asked.

Told her I was going to buy a car. I would need transportation when I finished school and went to work. I had only one semester to go in college before I became fully educated, as I then thought.

She wasn't enthusiastic about the car idea. One reason was, my father was driving a 1940-model Dodge at the time and it wasn't paid for yet. He was sixty-one, and had never driven a car that was paid for. I'm not sure he ever did.

My mother said there were things I could do with my money that would be better than buying a car. She said my father had been buying cars for half a century and hadn't gotten one paid for yet before it wore out. She liked my money where it was, in the bank, earning interest. She reminded me that even while I slept, my money was down there in the bank working. "It's growing *to* you," she said. "That's the thing to do. Put your money in something that will grow *to* you."

Grow to you. She loved those three little words, and stayed forever on the lookout for a way to get them into a sentence. The grammar of the phrase was archaic but it was clear enough what the words meant to her. She was captivated by the idea of owning something that increased in value all by itself and earned money even while she rested.

Livestock, for example. We would be rolling along the road in one of those old cars that wasn't paid for and she would see cows in a pasture and she'd say, "Now there's something that'll grow *to* you." Meaning that a calf will eventually become a valuable adult cow simply by eating grass, while its owner is nowhere near.

It made my father uncomfortable when she talked that way. He would go silent when she brought up the subject. He had never acquired anything that grew to him. His acquisitions grew the other direction, away from him. Like cars and clothes, that lost value every day instead of gaining it. I don't believe he *wanted* anything that grew to him. If he did I could never recognize the symptoms.

To ease my mother's mind about the money, I told her I wouldn't buy the car yet. I'd go on back to school and finish up and then I'd decide what to do about the money. She seemed relieved.

The spring term began in February which meant that I had more than two months to wait. I figured I had myself a vacation coming. I'd been in the Army three years without much time off. I went to the bank and got $200 and hit the road. I went to see old friends scattered throughout West Texas from Odessa to Fort Worth. The party lasted until after New Year's.

The following February when I went back to school, I was astonished to find myself broke. All 2,400 of those dollars, gone. I don't entirely understand yet where they went. Instead of growing to me, they had disappeared. It would be thirty years before I had that much money in the bank again.

I didn't tell my folks the money was gone. I borrowed enough from an old roommate to register, and later got a little help from the GI Bill. I finished up the spring of '46 with a BA degree in journalism from Texas Tech at Lubbock. The Lubbock *Avalanche-Journal* offered me a reporter's job at a salary of twenty dollars a week. I was insulted. I had picked up expensive tastes in the Army. I had already learned how to spend twenty dollars in one night in a bar in Los Angeles. I turned the job down.

Two months later I was wishing I had taken it, because I hadn't received a better offer.

The summer of '46, my father did me two giant favors. One was that he gave me a piece of advice. The other was that he made for me an extraordinary personal sacrifice. It may not seem so extraordinary when I tell you about it, but for him, it was. It was almost like giving me his life.

The advice came first. We were standing in the front yard of the little duplex apartment he and my mother were living in then, in Abilene. He had on his light gray suit and black shiny shoes. It was almost 1 P.M. and he was about to go back to work, selling men's clothing at Thornton's Department Store. I had just got home from looking for a job and I'd called him outside to tell him what my plans were. I expected that he'd be pleased. He was not.

I told him I wasn't having any luck getting a newspaper job and that reporter jobs didn't pay anything, anyway. I told him I had decided to stay home. I'd sleep on the back porch. I'd get some kind of work, maybe in the lumberyard. I'd worked in a lumberyard before. Even loading boards on a flatbed truck I could make more than twenty bucks a week. And staying home, I could save some money.

"I want to buy Mama a house," I told him.

The years I was off in the Army I often had fantasies about somehow getting hold of enough money that I could buy my mother a home. My folks had always rented, and a house was what my mother wanted above all else. In the fantasy I would see myself helping her into my new car. (I decided as long as I had all that money I might as well give myself a new car.) I would drive her out to the edge of town to a pretty little white house with green shutters. It would have a picket fence and a rock chimney. It would have a small pasture in the back where a Jersey cow grazed, with a new calf by her side.

I would say, "It's all yours, Mama. Your own house, at last. And it will increase in value the longer you live in it. It'll grow *to* you." Then I would hand her the keys.

What a hero I would be, and to my own mother. I could see the tears of gratitude streaming down that sweet person's face. It would be the best thing I'd done since I led her out of that flaming kitchen and saved her life, the night of the fire in 1927.

I would lie in my bunk and reenact that scene over and over. It would become so beautiful I would swear an oath that I would do it. Giving my mother a house would become my life's purpose, my goal. That money—which was then still in the bank—would be the down payment on her house.

But something always happened to change my plans. What usually happened was that I would fall in love. I had become an expert at that. I could go to a dance hall on the pike at Long Beach and dance with a girl I'd never seen before, and be a complete fool about her before we got twice around the floor. When I was in love that way, I would think about the little white house but instead of giving the keys to my mother I would give them to the girl. I bet I gave those keys to twenty different girls.

The day I told my father about my plan to stay home, I was in fact in love with a black-haired girl in the city of Breckenridge. This girl was something extraordinary. She wasn't just merely beautiful. In addition to that, her father was a rich oil man. The only trouble was, about a dozen other guys were also in love with her. Being in love with this girl was a co-operative project, combining the desperate efforts of guys scattered across six counties. I had been to her house when I had to stand in line to ring the doorbell.

Then one night she got married. Not to me, in case I need to mention it. I went to the wedding and sat in the losers' section. We made up a considerable gallery, every one of us feeling destroyed.

This was my condition when I made the decision to stay home and buy my mother the house.

My father heard me out, then rubbed his chin and jaw. That gesture meant he was about to say something deep and needed to think about how to say it. He would throw his jaw to one side, the way a man does when shaving, and rub his fingers along the skin as if he were checking for stubble. Finally he said, "Tell you what you ought to do. You ought not to stay here. You ought to get out. Go on, and find you a job and make your own life. You stay here, you might get stuck. You might never leave."

He walked to the car and started it and very nearly blew piston parts through the hood, racing the engine according to his old habit. Then he drove off to work.

I believe that was the best advice I ever received. I think he was seeing possibilities I couldn't see. Maybe he was seeing himself gone, and my mother a widow, and there I'd be, taking care of her, working at the lumberyard the rest of my time.

My feelings were hurt a little that he hadn't liked my selfless plan for buying that house. But they didn't hurt long. Couple of nights later I went out roaming around and came across a girl I'd gone to high school with. She was married but her husband was a long, long way off, still overseas. I didn't fall in love with her but I came close, and she helped me forget that sad wedding in Breckenridge.

Two weeks later, there was a phone call from one of the best friends I ever had, Professor Clark Schooley at Texas Tech. He had heard of a job, a sort of government publicity job. It meant writing press releases and it paid $200 a month.

"I'll take it," I said.

"Hold on. You'll have to apply. I understand a dozen people are after this job."

A dozen. The same number I was up against at Breckenridge, where I ran no better than sixth.

"I'll write a letter for you," Professor Schooley said. "I'll tell a couple of lies. It might help." Schooley was a good man.

The application form stated that the job would involve

travel and the applicant would have to provide transportation. "Do you own an automobile?" was one question on the form. I had to answer no. How was I going to buy a car? I owed money from my last stretch of schooling and I'd already tried and failed to borrow at the bank to buy clothes. I sat and stared at that "no" I'd written in response to the car question. Longer I looked at it the worse I felt. I got an eraser, changed the "no" to "yes," and mailed the application.

When they told me to come for the interview, I hitchhiked from Abilene to College Station, about 300 miles. I spent an afternoon on the campus of Texas A&M College with a gent named Louis Franke. We got along all right and at the end of the interview Franke told me he was fairly sure I'd get the job. "Stay close to the phone," he said.

We walked out of the building together. "Where are you parked?" he asked.

I told him over on the next street.

"Get in," he said, "I'll take you to your car."

I told him never mind, that it wasn't but a block or less and I could walk. He nodded and drove away and I hiked up on Highway 6 and began thumbing my way back to Abilene. I had never before been so aware of all those automobiles on Texas highways. Thousand of the things, and not one belonging to me.

Immediately after World War II, autos were not easy to buy. When the new '46 models began coming out, most went to the pre-war customers of dealers. Some people had been on dealers' new-car waiting lists all during the war, when manufacturers were making tanks and guns and GI trucks and not passenger cars. The price of cars remained under government ceilings for a while but many dealers would load vehicles to the scuppers with extra equipment so they could charge more than the basic ceiling price. A car was plainly out of my reach, even if I could have found one somebody would sell me.

I was faced with losing out on a plush $200-a-month job,

for the lack of a car. We talked the matter over at home. My father seemed to have a longer face about the problem than I did. I didn't understand why until the day Franke called and said the job was mine, to come on to work. My father walked around the house looking like a pall bearer. At the supper table he took the car keys out of his pocket and laid them by my plate.

"Here, you'll have to take the Dodge," he said.

Not once, not in my most desperate wanting of a car, had it even flickered across my brain to ask him to let me borrow that old Dodge. It was unthinkable. I could have as easily asked for his legs. You would have to know the man to understand fully the sacrifice he was making. If he had been a millionaire and said, "Here, take every dollar I've got," that wouldn't have been a greater act of charity.

I believe an automobile (and a good suit of clothes) is all he ever wanted to own. I do remember him saying one day that he'd like to own a saddle horse. But a car and a horse have in common what he valued—mobility. He had an itching foot. He loved going. I believe that if it hadn't been for our mother, who longed for permanency the way he did for the road, he would never have stayed more than six months in one place. The only reason he was working in that store was that during the war he couldn't get tires and gas for his traveling salesman job. That's what he was, more than anything else. A traveling salesman.

When I told him at the supper table that I wouldn't take the car, he said, "You'll have to. It's the only way. When you get on your feet and you're able to buy your own car, you can bring the Dodge back."

I believe my mother was glad about the car going with me. She had always hated his traveling. So did I, when I was growing up. It seemed he was always in Amarillo or somewhere when we needed him.

The morning I left, he helped me take my stuff out and load it in the Dodge. We didn't talk. We seldom did when things got tense. He stood way back, near the door, when I started the engine. I gave the gas pedal a deep stomp, to make the engine roar the way he always did it. I watched to see if he'd grin. He did not.

For the next year, he was without wheels. This proud, poor, well-dressed man, without transportation. Sometimes he walked to work. *Walked.* Sometimes he rode the bus, or hooked rides with neighbors. All that while, I was rolling around the state in his beloved Dodge, burning a quart of 40-weight oil every 200 miles, getting myself established to make a living writing sentences. Daily I would think of his face as I remembered it when I drove away from the house that morning. He looked abandoned.

A number of people have denied themselves in order to help me. But I can't think of a greater sacrifice made in my behalf than my father's letting me take his car. To go on, as he said, to make my own life.

After that day, except for short visits, I never went back home.

Three-Base Hit

THE MOST IMPORTANT EVENT in my personal history was a three-base hit. It happened in 1907, fourteen years before I was born.

The hit occurred in a pickup baseball game on the campus of John Tarleton Agricultural College at Stephenville. A tall skinny young fellow lined a pitch into the hole in left-center. I can see him running the bases, rounding second wide, knees and elbows pumping. He slid into third on his back in a cloud of red dust and a shower of gravel.

At that moment the doctor's daughter was strolling past the baseball field with a classmate. "Who is that?" she asked, meaning who was the fellow standing on third dusting off his pants.

He was the young man who would become my father in 1921. The doctor's daughter became my mother and so you can understand why I class that triple the most important hit ever recorded in baseball. If my father had fanned, or popped to third, I would probably not now be a member of the human race.

My parents were born within thirty miles of one another, a common circumstance in Texas in the late nineteenth century. In fact, thirty miles was a long way for a fellow to go looking for a wife. Most people married neighbors that they could see from the front porch.

My father did most of his growing up on a farm near the country town of Gordon, on the T&P Railroad sixty miles west of Fort Worth. My mother was reared in Stephenville, where her last name was Oxford.

It took me a long time to forgive her for that name. I didn't like it. When I heard it I always pictured an ox pulling a Model-T Ford. I didn't tell my mother that, though, because she was proud of the Oxfords. She would say there was a famous university by that name over in England, and her family could be traced back to a connection with that institution. Maybe it could, but it never was. I felt it would be all right not to mention the matter again.

My mother was also extremely proud of her father, who was one of Stephenville's town doctors. I barely remember Grandfather Oxford but I know I was afraid of him. I believe the reason was rooted in a story I heard about his cutting off a man's leg on the kitchen table. It wasn't explained to me that this was done for medical reasons and I counted it a pretty awful thing to do. I imagined that if Grandfather Oxford ever got me in the kitchen he would chop my leg off.

In addition to his last name, he had a first one I didn't like any better. It was Lafayette. When you went to school and got asked who your grandfather was, Lafayette just wasn't the kind of name you wanted to give. Everybody else had grandfathers called Walter, Richard, John, and even Willie.

In my stack of family keepsakes I have a photograph of Dr. Oxford. He shows a broad face and bright piercing eyes and great heavy shoulders. Also lots of hair, including a thick mustache. He appears to be what people used to describe as a "fine-looking man," which generally meant overweight. But being overweight in those times was fashionable and looked on as a sign of good health. Dr. Oxford died in 1926.

His wife was Nancy Melissa Hastings. They had nine children. Grandmother Oxford was known to us all as Maimie, a name I always had trouble spelling because we pronounced it Mammy. I remember her as quiet and gentle and thoughtful.

I once heard her say that a mesquite tree was pretty, and I

thought that was passing strange. I had never before heard anybody make a favorable remark about a mesquite. I grew up in mesquite. It was the commonest tree I knew the first twenty-one years of my life. It was full of awful thorns. The bark was so rough you couldn't climb a mesquite without losing part of your hide. The tree was all right for fence posts but not really of any account for shade. My father had a little joke about the man who died of sunstroke while sleeping in the shade of a mesquite.

More than twenty years after Maimie made the remark about mesquite, I saw one day that she was right. In the spring when those ferny leaves are washed by showers and take on a pale green shade, they're beautiful indeed.

Grandmother Oxford died in our house. She had been sick a long time and had come to live with us and one day she slipped and fell and broke her hip, and died.

My father's father was Harvey B. Hale. He was dead before my father was grown but I have long nursed the idea that I would have loved him and been close to him. Pictures of him remind me a little of Abe Lincoln. He was spoken of so infrequently when I was growing up that I began to suspect a smokescreen of some sort. There was something really interesting about Grandfather Hale that nobody was telling.

So I decided for myself what it was. I programmed into my computer all the shadowy hints I'd gotten that he had a fondness for the jug. Maybe the old itching foot, as well. He was a farmer but I got clues that he was not always on the farm when there was farming that needed doing. Yet I liked him without knowing why, and felt near him, a man who was dead long before I was born.

Of all my forebears that I never met or knew only briefly, Grandfather Hale is the one I would most like to meet now. I would love to hear him talk. Watch him eat and walk and ride a horse. Touch his hand. Did he chew tobacco? Did he tell jokes about mesquite shade? Could he play the harmonica? Did he stomp the floor early in the morning to make his shoes go on? Could he have passed on to a son the hankering to stay on the move? A reluctance to put down roots? Could he have passed on to a grandson a curious talent for spending money? And could that characteristic be sufficiently pronounced to inspire the expenditure of 2,400 precious dollars on a party spanning two months and stretching all the way from Odessa to Fort Worth? I think yes, to all those questions. There is no proving I'm right, or wrong, either.

Grandfather Hale's wife was Miley Ann Dickerson.

He left her with seven children, although I think some of them were gone from home when he died. This woman was known to me and a multitude of kinfolks as Grandma Hale. She stayed on the farm and operated it until her death. That piece of land is still widely known as Grandma Hale's Farm. It is no longer in the family, as we say. A lot of valuable property is no longer in our family.

I see Grandma Hale in a long print dress and a shawl and a lacy drawstring cap covering her hair. I see tiny kind eyes behind gold-rimmed spectacles, and a sweet little smile. In this vision I have of her, she seems frail.

But she had to be a strong woman, a matriarch.

The record is dim but it seems clear to me Grandma Hale took her children into Stephenville now and then to go to school for at least part of a year. It's certain that my father was going to school in town when he was thirteen because I have the original of a short composition he wrote that year as an assignment. The composition is done with a scratchy pen staff and is now framed and hangs on my wall and it's one of the dearest things I own. A deep sadness had touched him the night he did this assignment. I have long speculated that his spirit was low because things weren't right at home, and the lost traveler calling for help in his composition was his father. (You will see that he wasn't showing much promise as a speller.)

Composition About Everything

On the night of Dec. 6, 1899 I sat in my room thinking about what to write for a composition. I could see the light in the college and could hear the band playing. I could hear trains roaring. I could hear men and boys whistling and hollowing. I could hear the fire in the stove crackling and hissing. I could hear some body in an other room from me playing on an organ. Who every it was was playing 'Old Time Religion' and 'Gesus Now Is Passing By.' I could see all the dark clouds prevailing over us not a star was to be seen. The night was so dark it made me think of a cold winter night and the noises that I could hear called to my mind some poor persons voice who had lost his way on a cold snowy night and was calling for help. But at last every thing was calm and quite. I closed my composition with a fare well to all my friends school mates and play mates who were writing a composition. For every and for every Remember the night of Dec. 6, 1899. It was a very sad night to poor honorable Fred Hale.

Almost exactly two years after those lines were written, Grandfather Hale died. He was fifty-two. Grandma Hale had to be the one who saved that little composition. It's interesting to me that of all my father's homework, this is the only paper she saved. I wonder if she saw in it what I do—the death of her husband. First the sad calling for help by the lost traveler, and finally silence, "calm and quite."

The Mirrors

NEAR THE BACK DOOR of the First Methodist Church in Stephenville there was once a little frame house. I was born in that house on May 30, 1921. I believe my mother felt privileged to have a baby in the shade of a church, especially since it was Methodist. All the time I was growing up, the place of my birth was never mentioned without a reference to its proximity to a place of worship. At one point I began to feel that my principal distinction was being born up against a church. I always imagined, seeing they spoke of it so often, that the family liked living in that little house. In recent times my sister Maifred confessed to me she was glad when we moved. Because the church didn't have any plumbing and members of the congregation were always filing in and out of our house to go to the toilet.

The first public place I visited was that church. I was given what the Methodists call an infant baptism there, a good while before I began remembering things as well as I do now. About a quarter of a century afterward, I would get married to a pretty Baptist Sunday School teacher and I agreed to join her church in a sort of matrimonial way. She did not think a few drops of water on a baby's head was enough to have any effect. "What good does it do to baptize a little baby? He's not going to remember it. The Methodists are baptizing the wrong people. They ought to be baptizing the parents, not the babies." So I got baptized again, the second time Baptist style, in a tank of water and I was put full under in front of a large audience and I guarantee you I remember it.

But getting back to Stephenville, where my parents did a dreadful thing to me. They named me Carol. When I got old enough to see what they had done, I traced this felony to a certain music teacher. The family was fond of her. Her name was Carole. They wanted to name me after that lady. She told them, "The masculine form of the name is Carol, without the e." So that's what they put on my birth certificate. For more than forty years that name was a curse to me. I am not mad about it any longer. It's hard to stay mad all your life about a name.

I didn't know it at the time they were naming me but I wanted to be called Fred, my father's name. Somebody told my parents, "Don't name him Fred. He'll go through life being called Junior." I don't know who said that but I bet it was that meddlesome music teacher. I had a lot rather be called Junior than Carol. Or Leon, for that matter. They got that from my mother's first name, Leona. I feel as if I disliked the name Leona even before I knew my mother had it. My guess would be that Grandfather Oxford named her. Because I can't imagine that a thoughtful lady like her mother would name a tiny baby Leona. Grandmother Oxford had a beautiful name, Nancy Melissa, yet her daughters ended up with Leona May and Addie Lee. Would their mother have done that to them? Maybe so. Parents often commit dark sins in the matter of naming children.

I've always heard it was my father's idea to name me after my mother. It's curious to me, though, that he searched twenty years for something to call me other than the names on my birth certificate. I was wearing a size 11 shoe by the time he quit calling me Sonny Boy. My sisters never called me anything but Little Brother until I got a foot taller than they were. I didn't mind it. I liked it.

The best name our parents ever thought up was Maifred, for their first child. It's a combination of their own given names, May and Fred, and I think it's pretty and distinctive, even though a few people with a poor ear for names will call her Winifred.

My other sister was named for Little Ruth, our mother's younger sister who died as a small child. I don't know where the Ima came from. My father always called her Ima Ruthie and so do I, still, because that's who she is.

We moved from Stephenville when I was five. All that time in the town of my birth, I did nothing of importance. I initiated no event of any significance, although I did witness a few. I saw the rooster swallow the ring, for example. Saw my sister walking in her sleep around the courthouse square in the rain. Saw the eyes of the Booger Man in the Homeyers' garage. Saw Ima Ruthie playing Brahms at the age of four, and that was about it.

Each of these events I witnessed when we lived in different houses because we were always moving. We would be in a house for a year and one morning our mother would say we were moving and we'd gather up and go to another house. I can't remember thinking this was extraordinary. If I thought about it at all, I just thought it was the way people lived.

But I didn't imagine that they ever moved from one town to another. When I was five, they told me we were moving a long way off, to a place called Hamlin. My father had a shot at a better job in a distant city. He had to go there right away. We would come along later, when the movers loaded our possessions on a truck. The plan was that our mother would drive the car and follow the truck.

A weakness in that plan was that she couldn't drive.

Never mind, she said, she would learn. And she did, sort of. By the time the truck was loaded, she could drive a car pretty well but only in a forward direction. She hadn't yet learned to back up. She wasn't concerned about that. She didn't much believe in reverse, anyhow. She said:

"From here to Hamlin is straight ahead all the way. Why would I need to back up?"

That is one of the best things I ever heard our mother say, and my sisters don't remember it.

The distance from Stephenville to Hamlin, by way of the

muddy roads in 1926, was something like 150 miles. We were in an old touring car. The weather was windy and wet. We had to put up what we called rain curtains. In addition to three frightened offspring, our mother had in that car a Persian cat, a canary in a cage, and four goldfish in a half-gallon fruit jar. She had never driven an automobile except along College Avenue in Stephenville. I think of her now as a latter-day pioneer lady, pushing on into the West. The frontier women who went west in covered wagons had to endure Indian attacks and rattlesnakes and our mother didn't have to worry about those. But she had to contend with flat tires and overheated radiators and truck wrecks. No covered-wagon pioneer woman had to pick up after an overturned truck.

The truck that turned over was the one we were following, the one carrying our stuff. We came around a curve and there was the truck sprawled on its side in the ditch and all our possessions distributed over half an acre of hay meadow four miles east of Cross Plains.

Both my sisters began sobbing with enthusiasm when we caught up to the wreck. My recollection is that I felt mainly embarrassment, because of the public display of our belongings. We had a few nice things but most were not so nice that we wanted them exhibited. We had sensitive items on that truck. One was my personal mattress. It was lying against a barbed wire fence showing stains where I had wet the bed before I was housebroken.

It turned out that the driver had been trying to light a cigarette when he lost control and flipped into the ditch. This became important in our lives. My mother seemed to view the wreck as Divine Confirmation that she was justified in her view of the tobacco habit.

Even before the wreck, she believed that the reason lives were ruined, the reason people went to hell when they died, was connected firmly to smoking cigarettes and drinking whiskey. In the wreck she was presented with proof that the cigarette-half of her position was sound. If the driver hadn't been a smoker, he would not have been lighting a cigarette and he wouldn't have lost control and her belongings would not have been spilled into a muddy ditch. If she could have uncovered a clue that the driver had also taken a drink before he struck that match, her position would have been set in concrete. Her Compleat Guide To Human Ruination would have been demonstrated in one upended truck.

But the cigarette alone was enough to sustain her to the end of her life. Not one of her children will touch a cigarette today. For a good many years one of them did (never mind which one), but not now. Almost sixty years after that wreck, I am still influenced by it. When an eighteen-wheeler passes me on the interstate going seventy miles an hour, and if I see the driver digging in his shirt pocket for a smoke, I expect that when I make the next curve I will find his rig on its side in a pasture.

The wreck also gave us a family joke, a private expression that's still in use. When we got moved into the new house in Hamlin, there was a drawer missing in one of our dressers. It had somehow been lost when the movers were picking up the spilled furniture after the wreck. It was a bottom dresser drawer, and what was in it nobody knows. But forever afterward, when we couldn't find something we remembered having, we just said, "I guess it's in the bottom dresser drawer."

Our mother finally learned how to get the car in reverse and back it up. But not with much accuracy. The house in Stephenville where I was born was torn down. As near as I can tell, the place it stood is now a concrete parking lot. The church is still standing and has restrooms now.

We lived in Hamlin about a year. An important thing I learned there was how to cry almost as well as my sister Ima Ruthie. I have to say almost because she was an accomplished crier. She was always busy. When she wasn't laughing or singing or dancing or playing the piano, she was generally crying.

One time we had this pet chicken and it died. I was not as attached to that bird as Ima Ruthie was. She always had a deep feeling for any living thing, and if it suffered, so did she. If it

died, she grieved. I don't care what it was. It could be a lizard
and she would grieve about it.

This pullet I am talking about had a bad leg and it was let
into the house. I don't remember why but I will bet you a
blackland farm it was because Ima Ruthie cried in its behalf
until my father let her bring it in. He couldn't stand to hear
her cry.

As near as I could see, all the chicken ever did was stand on
one leg on the back porch, go peep-peep-peep, look pitiful,
and make messes. But Ima Ruthie counted that thing a fine
bird, and petted it, and tried to make it eat. It died anyhow
and she went into mourning. I went with her. She was two
years older and in those times we operated on seniority. You
followed the lead of the person just older than you were.

I didn't feel that much pain about the chicken. I had seen
chickens get their necks wrung ever since the rooster ate my
mother's wedding ring. But I had respect for Ima Ruthie's
tears, and I was good about helping her cry. I didn't always
understand why she was crying but even then I knew this:
She wasn't faking. If a stray cat got run over out on the road,
and she cried about it, those weren't phony tears. She cried
because she felt diminished by the death of that creature.

So I helped her grieve over the dead chicken and we gave it
a funeral in the back yard. This was the first of several animal
funerals I would assist her with.

Hamlin was a brief chapter in our lives. Toward the end of
it, I heard my father say the words "bad year" to another
man, and I wondered how a year could be bad. He was, of
course, talking about business. Something had gone sour
about the economy of West Texas and that new job that was
supposed to make him so much money didn't work out. He
took another job in a store in the nearby town of Stamford.
Stamford was a bigger town than Hamlin but the move didn't
improve our fortune. The fact was we had begun a slow roll
downhill, financially. I am thankful now that my parents
didn't know how far down we would roll.

——————————————————— ■ ———————————————————

A satisfactory thing that happened in Stamford was that I broke my arm. I liked having a broken arm because people began paying attention to me. One of the best ways a small kid can get attention is to go around with splints and a cast on his arm. Wonderful questions are asked, such as, "How did you break your arm?" And sometimes people would even listen to the answer.

A girl named Mary Beth Moody helped me break that arm. She lived near us and was Ima Ruthie's age and she played with us a lot. We played a curious game sometimes. We called it airplane crash, or something similar. One person was the airplane pilot and another was the crasher, or the catapult. The pilot sat on the upturned bare feet of the crasher, who lay in a tuck position in the grass. Then the crasher gave the pilot a great push by straightening the knees and catapulting him as far as possible. Mary Beth was the crasher and she gave me a good long fling and I landed wrong with my arm beneath me and I heard this little click. That was the bone breaking.

I don't remember that it hurt a lot but Ima Ruthie began to cry and so did Mary Beth and so I joined in, and a doctor came to our house to set the arm. He gave me chloroform, a scary experience. It made me see lions and tigers with fire coming out of their mouths when they roared.

But overall, I enjoyed the broken arm because my sisters and my mother were forever asking, "Does it hurt much?" I would reply that it hurt, sure, but it wasn't anything that I couldn't stand. I loved the painful expression on their faces. Ima Ruthie cried every night about my arm and by the time it healed we had that wonderful fire, so I had a very good year in Stamford.

With one exception: Stamford was where I found out that I was a funny-looking kid. I had these great ears growing in all directions. Men walking to work would come along and grin and say to me, "Hello, Ears. Where's the boy?" I asked my mother what they meant by that and she would say not to pay any attention to it, that men were always teasing children and it didn't mean anything. She said, "Don't ever let anybody tell you that you have funny ears. They're *good* ears."

About this time my sisters acquired a combination of mirrors of the kind girls want when they are getting particular about how they look. They could stand before one mirror and look into another and see how they looked from behind or from the side. They seemed pleased to have such an arrangement of mirrors and talked about it at supper.

One day when they were gone I went into their room to see why they were so fond of two ordinary mirrors. I had never found any use for mirrors.

A strange little person was in that room. He stood behind and a little off to the side of me. He wore my overalls. My shirt. My tennis shoes. When I moved my arm, he moved his. I suddenly squatted, and he squatted exactly when I did.

He looked nothing like me. I already knew how I looked and I was fairly handsome. My mother had told me I was. So had my sisters. My father hadn't mentioned it but he was so busy with other matters that he didn't have time to tell me.

I studied that kid in the mirror. He was pretty strange. He consisted mostly of skull, ears, elbows, kneecaps, and feet. He had this wide, sort of knobby forehead. His skull was too big for his skinny body. His eyes were too wide apart, and they didn't match up some way. This kid was a physical disaster and I certainly didn't intend to have anything to do with him.

So I went out of that room and left him behind and from that time forward, I avoided mirrors. If I wanted to know how I looked I would ask my mother. Sometimes when I was in a store or walking along a street downtown, a mirror would catch me off-guard and I would get a glimpse of the weird boy from my sisters' room. When that happened I would look another way and pretend I didn't see him.

In Stamford I was permitted to walk alone all the way to town to see my father in the store. I wore black and white tennis shoes and I liked the way they moved me along. I can see their rounded toes alternating in black and white flashes. I watched my toes all the way to town. I walked that way often—looking down. Maybe it was a way of avoiding mirrors.

Or avoiding cracks in the sidewalk. I had heard the saying, "Step on a crack, break your mother's back." I was fairly sure I couldn't break my mother's back by stepping on a crack but the notion stayed in my head because of a thing she would often say at night when she was tired. When the kitchen had been cleaned up after supper she would collapse on the old sofa and say, "My back is simply breaking," meaning that it was hurting. I knew it was just a manner of speaking and yet I never heard her say it without thinking that one of us had stepped on a crack that day. I got good at timing my stride to miss cracks.

I liked going to the store. It smelled so good, like cedar floorsweep. My father was important there, and handsome and smart and funny. I would half-hide behind a counter piled high with piece goods and watch him work.

He was seldom still, even when he wasn't busy. He did his work with a kind of flourish. I wish you could have seen him wrap a package for a customer. All purchases were wrapped then, not stuck into bags. A clerk needed to be a good wrapper.

When I watched my father sell, I always hoped for shoes so I could see him wrap them. The smooth way he tore the wrapping paper off the huge roll was wonderful, and he always tore off just enough, and slapped the box down in exactly the right spot on the paper, and folded it so precisely and quick around the box, and reached for the string without even looking. Later on when I began going to rodeos and watched the calf-ropers and saw the way they tied the legs of the calves so swiftly and with such style, I would think of my father wrapping a shoe box and tying it with string. When he finished he would place the box out on the edge of the counter, directly in front of the customer, and he would let it plop onto the counter and make a nice final noise. The customers liked that. It made them smile. It was a little show. He did all that wrapping and tying in one continual smooth movement, without a jerk or a second's hesitation.

But the best thing he did in the store was ride the rolling ladder.

Many dry goods stores and hardware stores in those times had merchandise shelved along the walls all the way to the ceiling. Ladders were built in so the clerks could reach stuff on the high shelves. At their bottoms the ladders had wheels that rolled along on metal tracks.

When he felt like showing off, which was fairly often, my father would swing onto a rolling ladder at the front of the store and shove off with a long leg and roll all the way to the shoe department in the back, grinning and waving. When he did that I could barely stand to keep quiet. I wanted to leap up and yell, "Looky there! That's my father! Isn't he something?"

He was fast with a wisecrack, too, and could keep everybody laughing when he was going good. Probably he ought to have been in show business. He was a good dancer and he could play the harmonica the same way Ima Ruthie played the piano and he could throw his voice. Other kids in the neighborhood would brag about how strong their fathers were. I would brag that mine could throw his voice across the street. Not another father in any town we ever lived in could do that.

The way he'd do it—say a person he knew pretty well would come in the store. Say it was John Brady. My father would turn his head toward the back of the store and produce this high-pitched, remote-sounding voice. It was like a person calling, loudly, from a considerable distance.

"John Brady! John? Oh John Brady!"

Mr. Brady would turn and go back outside and look across the street and all around, to see who was calling him in that somewhat urgent tone. Then the call would seem to come from a different direction, from the back of the store, and he would come back in, walking fast and looking so earnest and puzzled. The small audience that was in on the joke would begin snickering and at last somebody would explode into laughter and bring the stunt to an end. My father would stand there grinning and being a hero. I doubt Mr. Brady found much entertainment in my father's voice-throwing but a lot of people did and they were always requesting it.

In Stamford my father took me with him to open the store early in the morning a few times. His first duty was to sweep the walk in front of the store and put out the U.S. flag. It didn't strike me that the sweeping was menial work that a janitor might do. It seemed proper and important to me, especially since the sweeping was done in conjunction with raising the flag. I thought of it as cleaning the walk so it would be good enough for the flag to fly over.

I hadn't any way of knowing that he didn't really want to be working in a store, sweeping sidewalks. He wanted to be on the road, moving along. But I believe now that he tried to have as much fun in the store as he could because where else was he going to have any? He was spending his life in that place. His working hours were dreadful.

Up at 5 A.M. Milk the cow. To the store by 7. Home at noon for lunch. Back to the store by 1. Home again at 5. Milk the cow. Eat supper. Back to the store until 9, when it closed. Back home, to go to bed so he could get up at 5. I never have known a man who worked so hard, and accumulated less.

On one of the mornings he let me go with him to town, a special thing happened for the two of us. He opened the store and swept and brought out the flag. Every store had a brass socket set into the concrete of the sidewalk. The flagpole fit into that socket. He fitted it in, and unfurled the flag and a nice little breeze kept it curling and waving and it was really beautiful. The sun was coming over the store buildings and laying long shadows on the street. Not many other people were out yet and it was a pretty morning and our private time.

I felt he was about to tell me special things. Not in words. He didn't have the words. He put his great hand on my shoulder and pulled me close to him and that was extraordinary because he almost never touched me. Our family weren't huggers and kissers like some. He grinned down at me and looked back up at the flag and then I looked, too, and we stood there a little while, looking at the flag together.

He never made a sound but I decided to believe he was telling me he loved me, something he never said out loud. I decided also he was saying that things were all right, that I shouldn't worry, or be afraid. When he looked back down at me I could see the light glinting off the moisture in his eyes.

I loved everything about the store except the three-way mirrors, where customers in new suits and dresses stood and turned and studied themselves from various points of view. I hated the mirrors because the weird-looking kid was always in them, wearing my clothes.

Another event of significance in Stamford involved a little girl about my age. She lived near us and sometimes came over to play in our yard. I remember a certain dress she wore. It was dark brown, with a purple cast, and patterned with small white dots. I think what attracted her to the yard this day was that my father had brought home several large cardboard packing crates.

The crates made fine building materials. They could be put together to form forts, rooms, tunnels. Some were so large we could stand up in them. In the biggest one she said to me, "Look." She raised her dotted brown skirt and pulled her panties down and afforded me a thorough examination (visual only) of all the territory her underwear normally covered. I had asked for no such privilege but I took it.

"There it is," she said.

There it was, indeed. I couldn't imagine that anything needed to be done about it, and nothing was. But I felt a curious heat in my face and a thumping in my chest and a tingling in my neck and a weakness in my legs and so I supposed that I was seeing something really important.

Then we moved to Fort Worth.

Fort Worth

I STOOD BEFORE *my classmates in Miss Hettie Green's first grade room and I gave this wonderful, forceful speech. I was confident and composed. I did not fidget. I did not pull at my ears or twist my neck or look down at my feet. I spoke out against arithmetic. I said arithmetic was all right for counting marbles or jawbreakers but beyond that it was mainly useless and we ought not to fool with it any longer. I said reading was not bad but we needed better stuff to read. No more stories about dumb families whose members said to each other such strange things as "The wind blows" and "The kite is high." I said also that the subject of drawing was satisfactory except why did we have to draw pictures of bears and Pilgrims. I said we wanted to draw things in Fort Worth where we lived, things we saw every day. When I finished and sat down, my classmates rose as one and gave me an ovation. It felt really fine, being a hero again.*

The population of Fort Worth, Texas, when we moved there in 1928 was something like 150,000. I had heard of the place, in the same way I had heard of New York and Chicago, but I'd never been there. I'd never been to any city. I was not prepared for anything the size of Fort Worth.

This is where I first began to understand that the Hales were country folks. Before Fort Worth, I had thought of us as town people, because we didn't live in the country the way Grandma Hale did. I considered Stephenville to be a city. It was a county seat and had a grand courthouse and it had a college. It not only had a Methodist church, it had the *First* Methodist Church. In my judgment, that meant it was the most important of all Methodist churches. I figured the Second Methodist Church was off somewhere in a town smaller than Stephenville, and the Third and the Fourth were in smaller places still.

When I discovered America there, Stephenville was actually a little country town of about 3,000 souls. Hamlin was even smaller and Stamford, our next stop, was near the same size. When we were in Hamlin my father would take me with him on Sunday afternoons and drive a little way outside of town and shoot prairie dogs from the car window with a .22 rifle. He would skin them and bring the meat home to feed to the cats. That colony of prairie dogs was probably not half a mile from our front door. Hamlin and Stamford were little rolling-prairie country towns in Jones County, north of Abilene. It wasn't possible to be citified while living in such towns, with a milk cow in a barn out back and chickens roosting in the trees. But I didn't realize that until we got to Fort Worth.

What a metropolis it was. Traffic lights. Flashing signs. Buildings soaring twelve and fifteen stories tall. Even streetcars, magnificent streetcars, popping and sizzling, giving off waterfalls of electric sparks, their wheels groaning and singing on the rails, their bells clang-clang-clanging. I supposed this was the most exciting and very likely the greatest city on the planet. For me, in fact, Fort Worth remained the Center of the Universe until I got out of high school, even though we stayed there only two years. It was a perfectly wonderful place.

It had not just a college but a university, Texas Christian. It had radio stations, daily newspapers, parks with zoos and ferris wheels and concrete swimming pools. It had a great public library with a Chinese coolie, made of wax, standing inside the front door. Where else could you find such a thing? There were also several large hospitals. Soon I would spend some time in one, and have a reunion with those fire-breathing lions and tigers I had met in the chloroform dream when I broke my arm.

But best of all, Fort Worth had a professional baseball team, the Fort Worth Cats of the Texas League. The best baseball team in the world.

The main reason we moved to the city was so my sister Maifred could go to TCU. There was no way she could have left home to attend college. We simply didn't have the money for that kind of thing. Besides, my parents thought she was too young to leave home. She was swift in school and had graduated from Stamford High when she was barely seventeen, before I had started the first grade. I was pushing eight before they ever got me in school, and I wasn't eager to go even then.

We moved into a red brick duplex apartment not far from the TCU campus and just across the street from George C. Clarke Elementary. I had to walk a couple of hundred yards from our front door into the first grade classroom of Miss Hettie Green. I liked Miss Green all right but I hated being so near home. At recess I could sometimes see my mother standing on our front porch, watching me. One day she showed up on the schoolground to bring me a jacket, just as if she didn't know she was committing an unforgiveable sin. We were all standing in line so every kid in school was watching, to see which titty-baby had to have his mama bring him a coat, and it was me, and I was mortified.

I wanted to tell her if she ever came on that schoolyard another time for any reason, I would never speak to her again. No, wait, I would run off from home and I wouldn't come back. But I didn't say it. I couldn't.

That was our way, not to talk about painful matters, the very ones that needed talking about. Instead we crammed them inside us and let them collect and compact. This was one of the disadvantages of loving one another so much.

We couldn't bear to say a thing that might wound sensitive feelings.

When I visited in the homes of friends and heard the way boys talked to their mothers, I was astonished. It frightened me. I thought God would bring down an awful punishment on those boys and I might get caught in it. One day I heard a friend shout at his mother, "I hate you!" I felt like diving for the ditch, for surely a bolt of lightning would strike him dead for issuing that blasphemy.

Later on I found out it's common for angry children to shout those words at their mothers. But I promise you it would have been uncommon at our house. I can't recall ever raising my voice in anger to either of my parents, not once, in all the time I was growing up, and I am certain my sisters didn't. I believe both our parents went on to their graves without ever being spoken to harshly by their children. When I tell that to people they often say, "That's just wonderful." But I'm not sure. I think maybe we'd have been better off if we'd yelled now and then, or at least been able to argue and criticize with enthusiasm and feeling.

We haven't changed. Since 1946 I have written a daily newspaper column and now six books, counting this one, and neither of my sisters has ever made one negative comment about anything I've written. Along the way I've managed on occasion to crank out some perfectly awful stuff that must have disgusted or embarrassed them, but they didn't mention it for fear of wounding me. I believe their only criticism of my prose came back there in 1927 when they felt obliged to question my version of the house fire. Even that was done gently, and they hated to do it, I know.

Going to school in Fort Worth was not bad, except for arithmetic and drawing. I liked learning to read and my only complaint was they gave us such dull people to read about. The primers had mothers and fathers who didn't look or talk like any mothers or fathers known to exist in Texas, not even in Fort Worth. One primer I brought home had a boy of maybe seven or eight and he talked really funny. Like he'd point and say, "Oh, Father, Father, see the train. The train is long."

Which suggested that the father was retarded. If a train came along, no normal father would need to be told to see it. I brought this matter up at the supper table and was advised just to accept it, that sometimes we must simply accept things without question.

From the start, I had trouble with numbers in school but Miss Green somehow got the notion that I was good at them. She was a sweet lady but not a great judge of talent. She did something to me that made me hate arithmetic even more than when I was first introduced to it. Teachers can't know what brands they burn into the tender hides of little children.

She called three of us before the room to demonstrate how to count by threes. We were all boys, supposed to be sharp at number work. Girls were expected to be better at reading, and especially writing. One of the boys was my friend Carter who really was good with numbers. He also owned a small bicycle that I coveted. Call the other boy William. Miss Green stood us side by side—Carter, then William, then me—and we were to count by threes for the edification of the class.

That is, Carter would start with 3. Then William would say 6. Then I was supposed to hit 9. Well, I couldn't see how it worked, and I had to be told. The next time my turn came I was due to say 18 but I panicked and all I could do was guess and I guessed 20, or something wrong like that. We stayed before the class all the way to 100 and I didn't hit the right number one time and I was destroyed because everybody kept laughing at me. And afterward a kid came up to me and gave me the news that my ears didn't match, that one was bigger than the other and grew crooked.

That was a bad experience and I wanted to go home and give up school altogether. I laid the fault to numbers, to arithmetic. I told myself if I just stayed away from arithmetic I wouldn't ever get into a mess of that sort again.

I was better at drawing. Miss Green was forever making us draw bears, in connection with that Goldilocks story. I felt it was curious that we were required to draw only what was unfamiliar to us. I mean how many West Texas children had ever seen a bear in the woods? In 1928 we did in fact have bears in Texas, and still do in places out west of the Pecos River, but no bears were going to live anywhere close to a prairie town like Fort Worth. A bear wants trees.

But Miss Green kept us on bears, and Eskimos. Also Pilgrims, and Indians in Minnesota.

Why didn't she let us draw what we knew about? Why not the magnificent Percheron that pulled the milk wagon through our neighborhood early every morning and made those deep rich *clop clop clop* sounds with his great shod hooves? Why not the grandstand at LaGrave Field where the Fort Worth Cats played? How about the wax Chinaman inside the door of the library? Or the pens and the cattle at the stockyards that smelled so fertile in north Fort Worth?

But no, we were required to do Pilgrims and Eskimos and those Minnesota Indians making canoes out of birch bark. Few states have more Indian history than Texas but for years I failed to develop any interest in Indians because I thought they all lived up in Minnesota.

Still, I was never in a classroom where I learned more in nine months than I did in Miss Green's in 1928 and '29. Fifty years after I walked out of that room I went back and stood in it awhile, because so much of what happened there was significant in my life. For example, it was the place where I first fell in love.

With an orange girl.

She sat across the aisle from me. Her hair was called red but it was not, it was orange. She was orange everywhere. Her face, all her skin, had a wonderful pale orange cast. Her eyes couldn't have been orange but they seemed to be when the light came off her hair in just the right way. If you had asked me at this time what my favorite color for eyes was, I would have said orange.

On Valentine's Day, according to the Law of Miss Hettie Green, every pupil in the room exchanged handmade Valentines with everybody else. So you got out your construction paper and your little scissors and your paste and Crayolas and you made twenty-five Valentines and gave them out, and you got twenty-five in return. I got a shock when I opened the Valentine from the orange girl. She had written in it, "I Love You."

The biggest mule in Tarrant County could have kicked me and I wouldn't have gotten a greater impact than I got out of those three words. I bet I gasped. The same heat I felt in the packing crate in the back yard in Stamford rushed to my face. I put the Valentine in my primer. Every few minutes I would crack the book a little way and peek again at the words to see if they were still there. I took them home. Took them to the bathroom. Took them to bed with me.

You understand that the orange girl had written the same message to everybody in the class, including Miss Green, but I didn't think of that. I wouldn't have seen what it meant even if I had thought of it. I trotted right off into love with that orange girl and stayed for weeks and weeks.

It had no effect on her, however, for the reason that I didn't tell her. It was way too personal a matter to talk about. That established for me a pattern that would last for many years— falling in love with girls and not telling them. I didn't tell them because I didn't imagine they would be interested in knowing it. I figured no pretty girls were going to have an interest in a boy with crooked ears and weird eyes. Why would they?

One reason it was so easy to fall in love with the orange girl was that my resistance was low. I had been sick, and I have to say that my sickness might have been traced to the Law of Miss Hettie Green. One paragraph of the Law stated that every pupil would keep a health chart. Which was probably a good idea but I took the Law too seriously.

The chart had blank squares to represent the various items of health responsibility. That is, there was a square to show whether you brushed your teeth. Whether you drank milk. Whether you ate vegetables. Whether you had taken a bath. Whether you had exercised. If you had done those things, you were entitled to color in the squares that corresponded to them. Every child wanted to come to school with all squares on his chart colored, to show how healthy he was.

There was a square for sleeping with a window open. The Law counted it healthy to sleep with lots of fresh air pouring in. But my mother balked on that one. I was sleeping then on a narrow cot jammed up against two windows. We were tight on space in that apartment, with five of us living there, and my cot wouldn't fit any other place. My mother was opposed to my sleeping with my nose in an open window. I had shown talent for ear infections, so when I would open a window she would close it and I'd have to go to school with the fresh-air square uncolored on my health chart.

That was an embarrassment so I began cheating in favor of the health chart. When everybody else went to bed I would open the window a little way and sleep there with my head practically outdoors, even during the coldest nights. In winter, when the polar fronts sweep down off the Great Plains, Fort Worth can get bitter cold. One night in the fall of '28 we had a norther that must have come straight off the Artic Ice-cap. Sleeping in the window that way I developed the grandfather of all ear infections.

They took me out of school. They began driving me often to downtown Fort Worth to a doctor who rammed awful probes deep into my ear and it hurt like hell and I did a lot of yelling about it. I didn't get any better. I kept running a high fever and having outrageous dreams. Finally they told me I had developed mastoiditis and would need an operation.

I decided I was going to die. The lions and tigers returned to my dreams. They snarled, and prowled, and showed their awful claws and teeth. Even when I was awake, I heard doom-sounds:

"Gong! . . . Gong! . . . Gong-gong! . . ."

Across the street on the schoolyard stood a wicked item of playground equipment called a Giant Stride. That was the source of the sounds that I associated with dying. I thought the name of it was Giant's Ride. It was constructed on the order of a maypole, except it was iron. Its heavy center post was set in concrete. A sort of wheel, or disc, rotated on top of the post. Descending from the disc were chains, equipped at their lower ends with ladderlike hand-holds for the children.

Each child would grab a chain by the hand-hold and run around and push out, and up, in this way take giant strides, which I suppose is where the name of the thing came from. You can understand that if one child let go when the rig was rotating, a chain with three rungs of an iron ladder would be left flopping and swinging and looking for a way to hurt somebody.

If a child, unaware of the danger, wandered near the thing when it was spinning, he was a candidate for an ambulance ride. I once saw a little girl catch one of those flailing chains in the face and it was surely an unhappy event. Why school authorities allowed such equipment on a campus is a mystery.

When I was sick and having all that fever and a norther was scouring the schoolyard across the street, the loose chains of the Giant Stride would swing in the wind and the iron handles would bang against the great hollow metal pole. Far into the night the sound would reach me in my bed and it would be distant and terrible.

"Gong! . . . Gong-gong! . . . Gong! . . ."

Half-awake, half-dreaming, I recorded that sound as the Voice of Doom.

They took me to the hospital and this time it wasn't chloroform, it was ether. The lions and tigers were more agitated by ether than they were by chloroform. They fought and clawed and roared and shot flames from their mouths and eyes, like pictures of dragons I had seen. The doctor chiseled into the mastoid bone behind my right ear and removed the part of it that was infected and inflamed and eventually I got all right again.

But that doctor laid a sentence on me. He said that for the rest of my life I would need to protect my head because I had a hole in my skull behind my ear and if I got a solid lick at that point it could be serious. It could kill me. *That* serious. I was not to play football, or get into fist fights, or butt my head into solid objects.

Before I got the bandages off my ear, I was running after somebody in a game of chase and I stumbled and fell and hit my noggin on the corner of a concrete banister. I went home and showed the wound to my mother. My father was gone with the car. My mother wrapped a clean cloth around my head to stop the bleeding and secured the bandage with a safety pin. We walked three blocks and caught the Lipscomb trolley. On Hemphill we transferred to the big streetcar that took us downtown to the Medical Arts Building where the doctor sewed up my head. Eight stitches. We rode back home the same way and in time for my mother to fix supper. It was a good trip and we had fun. I didn't get to ride into town on the streetcar very often.

It seemed to me that after the doctor said not to get a lick on the head, I was always getting them.

The spring of '29 I graduated from Miss Hettie Green's first grade and said good-by forever to the orange girl. And I never again kept a health chart.

When we moved to Fort Worth my father quit the store business and went back on the road to do what he loved most— selling and traveling. He had been on the road several years before I was born, selling work clothes to dry goods stores. The reason he had quit traveling, he had been given the chance to work up and become the manager of a branch in a dry goods store company. After I was grown he told me he wasted a lot of time working in stores before he realized he would never make a manager. He didn't like to tell people what to do, and didn't like to fire anybody. So back to traveling.

I was never proud of what he sold when he traveled. He went to work for a company that manufactured machines that sat on store counters and dispensed paper tape for sealing packages. He called on the kind of stores he had worked in, where he had wrapped packages and tied them with string in such a pretty way. Now he was selling machines and rolls of gummed tape that would make obsolete his wonderful way of wrapping merchandise.

It is still my idea that he could have become rich if he had only sold the right thing, something big, like locomotives or office buildings or ranches and farms, because he was an excellent salesman. But to me he always seemed to be selling what nobody really wanted.

I never did like that company that made the tape machines. He worked for it strictly on commission and if he ever made a decent wage, I couldn't tell it. We seemed forever broke, and looking for a new place to live.

Before Christmas of '28 we moved out of the brick duplex and into an old frame house farther from school. I am pretty sure we moved because the rent was cheaper. That was always why we moved. The only other reason I can think of, sometimes we moved because there was a better place to keep a milk cow. But in the case of Fort Worth that reason doesn't apply because we never did have a cow in Fort Worth. Even my father saw it was not practical to have a cow grazing in the back yard in the middle of a city of 150,000 people.

You hear it said now that the Great Depression began with the stock market crash of 1929. But it began before that. For our family it began not long after we left Stephenville. We didn't know anything about stock market crashes. We didn't know what a stock market was, or how one could crash.

I hadn't recovered from the mastoid operation or the eight stitches in my forehead before I came down with whooping cough. Then I tried the measles, and so did Ima Ruthie. Christmas came and went and we didn't even know it. My sister Maifred told me in recent times that the Christmas of '28 was the only Christmas of her life that she did not receive a present, not one.

Those had to be desperate times for our parents. My mother would get me alone and talk to me about praying. She said I ought never to miss a day asking God to take care of us.

She helped me compose a prayer. It was in two parts. First

came the requests, and then came the thanks. I would start out by asking for help in being good, so I wouldn't tell fibs or take things that weren't mine or violate any of the Ten Commandments. Then I was to mention each member of the family and point out their particular problems and ask for speedy solutions. I prayed also for people outside the immediate family. We had a lot of relatives and it took time to cover them all.

My mother said that if I wanted a thing then I could ask God for it and if he thought I ought to have it he would get it for me. But he wouldn't give me a thing I wasn't supposed to have. I think what that meant was that it wouldn't be of any account to pray for Carter's bicycle, which is what I wanted more than anything.

In the second half of the prayer I was to thank God for a dozen or more blessings, and especially for my health. I didn't have a lot of enthusiasm about thanking him for my health in a year when I had survived a mastoidectomy, whooping cough, measles, and eight stitches in my forehead, but I did it anyhow to please my mother. I never did have the confidence in prayer that she did.

Something I was thankful for—I always forgot to thank God for this so I do it now, in print—my mother never made me say my prayers out loud. Some kids had to do that. I had visited in homes where mothers "heard" the prayers of their children, as if the children were praying to their mother instead of God and this made me uncomfortable. The nearest my mother came to that, she would drift silently to my bed and ask if I had said my prayers. Once I told her I was too sleepy to say them. She replied, "How can you expect God to help you if you can't stay awake long enough to send up your prayers to him?"

I saw she had a point. I developed a secret system to make certain I didn't miss any prayers. On nights when I wasn't very sleepy I would do the same prayer six or seven times, to get a jump on the game. It was a great luxury to fall in bed, drunk with sleepiness, and tell myself, "Don't worry about praying.

You're still two nights ahead." And fall asleep with a clear conscience.

But I didn't mind praying when I was alert. I sort of liked the idea of sending prayers up, as my mother said. I could see them rising. The words leaving me, going up through the ceiling, the roof, through the leaves of the hackberry trees. Prayerful words, snaking up through the night. ". . . and bless Uncle Barney, and Uncle Grover and Aunt Maude, and . . ." See them climbing, growing smaller and smaller as they got farther from Fort Worth and closer to heaven.

In the spring, things got to looking better. At least they did to Ima Ruthie and me. We never did know how bad they were, anyhow. As long as we weren't sick, we had a good time. It's a wonderful aspect of youth that the young can go on playing and laughing while their parents are in spiritual desolation.

There were bright spots that are good to remember.

Sometimes Uncle Barney Hale would come spend a few days with us. He was our father's younger brother, a genial loose-jointed, slump-shouldered fellow, full of silent laughter. I always felt that Uncle Barney knew extraordinary and humorous things that needed to be laughed about but he didn't laugh aloud because nobody else knew what the things were and wouldn't see why he was laughing. He was one of my favorite people.

He paid attention to me. He liked me. He never looked at me as if he thought I was some kind of curious bug, the way so many adults did. He called me Cowhand. I didn't know why and still don't, but I liked it. He would joke and laugh with Ima Ruthie and me, at a time when our father's cares had burdened him so that he couldn't laugh.

I never knew Uncle Barney to have a job, the way other men did. It was said he was a tool dresser in the oil fields. I didn't know what that meant but it sounded pretty neat. Dressing tools. It was also said that he was a professional gambler, which happened to be true. This wasn't talked about in our house but we all knew it. I was fascinated by it and sometimes I bragged about it.

Havings things to brag about was important then. Uncle Barney's being a gambler gave me material from outside the immediate family. He complemented my father, who could throw his voice across the street. My sister Maifred could walk in her sleep in the rain and recite a poem in Spanish. My sister Ima Ruthie could play the piano before she could reach the keyboard. My mother could slice a pie into five equal pieces.

The boast about the pie was not my personal observation. I think it originated with my father but I heard it from the time I began listening. I was grown and gone from home before I appreciated that being able to slice a pie five equal ways was something extraordinary, at that, and of significant value in a family of five people.

But Uncle Barney and his gambling, that was one of my foremost boasts. It always got attention. Boys two and three years older than I was would find it interesting. Not another kid in any of the neighborhoods we lived in had a gambler for an uncle.

In that strange year of 1928, kinfolks came frequently to our house to eat and sleep and we were not always glad to see them. But Ima Ruthie and I were happy to see Uncle Barney. He would take part in minor adventures with us.

Driving the old Chevy, for example, with an empty gas tank. That was the sort of thing we loved him for. Ima Ruthie and I thought that nobody else could have done it, and the day it happened became special in our lives.

"Going riding," is what we called it. Ima Ruthie and I never got enough of riding around Fort Worth, seeing the sights. It was a thing we often did on Sunday afternoons, until money got so tight our father couldn't buy gas for joy riding. On this particular day, he said the tank was empty and so there would be no riding. Uncle Barney volunteered to buy a gallon of gas, which cost probably less than twenty cents.

Our folks stayed home and Uncle Barney and Ima Ruthie and I set out in the Chevy. Uncle Barney had no car of his own then. I suspect he had lost it in a card game. I don't mind making that speculation because one time he confessed to me that he had *won* one in a card game. So it seems reasonable to suppose that he could lose one, as well.

He said to us, "Let's see how far she'll go before she runs out of gas." Meaning the Chevy with the empty tank. The gauge was showing empty. And in this way he made something exciting of a simple drive around town.

We went to TCU and chugged around the campus and exclaimed for the tenth time about the great buildings. We drove through Forest Park along the Trinity River Bottom. We went to Meacham Field to watch a tri-motored airplane take off and land. The gas gauge fell way below the empty mark and this made every mile, every block, every turn an adventure.

Once the engine sputtered and we squealed, knowing that this was it, she was dying at last. But no, the engine caught and the Chevy rolled on, and Uncle Barney shook with his silent laughter. We even went to town and got on the tracks behind an empty streetcar and followed it to the barn, to see where it stayed.

We must have driven fifty miles, long and slow and laughing miles, and that old car never did run out of gas and this was an afternoon that we would write themes about in school. It was just the sort of adventure we needed and loved, and Uncle Barney knew this.

He never stayed with us long. He knew how to visit. I couldn't have gotten it into words then but I somehow learned from him a valuable rule about visiting: The reason they're always glad to see you when you arrive is that the last time you were there, you left before they were ready for you to go.

We would be looking for him, to ask a question, or to show him a frog we had caught in a vacant lot, and he would be gone. He wasn't much on farewells. After one of his secret departures I went into the kitchen looking for him and two dollar bills were lying on the kitchen table. Money was never left around our house then, not even nickels. I asked my mother about the dollars and she said, "Barney left them."

From that incident it pleased me to conclude that when he came to our house and ate and slept when money was so scarce, he always left my mother enough to cover his expenses. I don't know that this is true. But I hope it is.

Two dollars covered a considerable lot of expenses the winter of '29. I remember going along with the Wilson brothers, older than I was, when they delivered the *Fort Worth Star-Telegram*. I went with them because they would let me. I wanted to be seen with them, to learn how to fold a paper for throwing, to be associated in some way with a profitable enterprise. Boys with paper routes were looked on with favor by their peers and their elders. It was said of the Wilson boys that they had good heads on their shoulders and would amount to something when they grew up. My mother was pleased that I associated with them.

One afternoon a man came up to us in the street and said he wanted a paper. The Wilsons always carried a few extra papers for possible street sales. They let me pull the paper out of the bag and hand it to the man and take the money—two cents. The older Wilson boy said to me, "Keep it. It's yours, for helping." I went home and told about selling the paper and showed the two pennies and everybody in the family looked at them with respect, and there were no indulgent smiles.

My mother said, "Why don't you save them? Ten of those make a dime, remember, and ten dimes make a dollar. Save them, and let them grow *to* you."

But I couldn't see it. Two pennies weren't enough to start anything with and the next day on the way to school I stopped at the store and spent them for Tootsie Rolls.

Our father had a way of working little miracles and getting things for us just when we needed them the most, and when they were impossible to get. In the depths of that winter of

'29, he got Ima Ruthie a ukulele. I have always wondered where it came from.

Ima Ruthie could play it, of course, without lessons or practice. She took it from our father and she hadn't ever seen a ukulele and she played "Springtime in the Rockies." Everybody smiled and patted their feet. We needed smiles and foot-patting then. Ima Ruthie sang the words, and knew them every one.

Near our house on College Avenue was a small city park. Capps Park. It had a brick-and-concrete stage at one end. No seats, no theater, just that stage. Ima Ruthie is the only person I ever saw perform on that stage. She would get up there with her ukulele and play and sing "Sidewalks of New York" and tap dance:

"East (tappy-tap) Side (tappy-tap) West (tappy-tap) Side (tappy-tap) All-l-l around thu town (tappy-tappy-tappy-tappy) . . ."

She would have an audience of one. Me. She needed an audience and so I sat out there and represented a great crowd.

Sometimes my mother's brothers came to stay with us. They would come two or three at a time and fill the house with smoke and conversation and importance.

Uncle Jay Oxford was the biggest of them. He was full of bluster and gave off loud noises. I was afraid of him. He never said anything to me. Sometimes he would stare at me from behind his thick hornrims and his expression would say, "What's that?"

Uncle Roy Oxford was tall and red with scaly skin. He talked about working in lumberyards but when he came to our house he was not working anywhere. I always thought he was stuck on himself for no reason that was apparent, but later on he would do me a great favor and help me get a job and so I am supposed to be indebted to him. Uncle Jay had no job, either, at this time, but he always had a big deal working that just hadn't materialized quite yet. He was waiting on a phone call all the time. Uncle Clay Oxford came, too, and I liked him. He had great strong hands and thick arms. He told stories about working in corn patches and wheatfields in Oklahoma, Kansas, Nebraska, Iowa, Indiana. So he was a farmhand, and followed the harvest. He told about entering corn-husking contests in the Midwest and I thought he was all right.

If it sounds as if all the men who visited us were out of work, that's because they were. The exception was Uncle Barney, who did not need a job. All he needed was a poker game.

My mother had other brothers who didn't run around the country visiting because they were working and taking care of families. Uncle Ray Oxford was a maintenance foreman for the Texas Highway Department and lived at Glen Rose, southwest of Fort Worth. I counted him a wonderful man, and handsome. He had lots of wavy hair and looked like Paul Muni, the movie actor. We did not know about Paul Muni in '29 but we did in the early '30s. I believe Muni's *I Was A Fugitive From A Chain Gang* was the first talking picture I ever saw.

Then we had Uncle Grover Oxford who was a cowboy and worked on ranches and ought to have had a ranch of his own. He was such a good man. He would be part of a painful drama that my family would endure on a sheep ranch the winter of '32. Through that experience I learned to admire and love that man.

When all the out-of-work Oxford brothers would come to see us at once, they would hump over the dining table after supper and play endless games of dominoes, and a card game called pitch. The air in the house would grow almost white with the smoke from their roll-your-own cigarettes. This is when my mother began lecturing me about the evils of the tobacco habit. She would walk frowning through the house, flailing her hands to dispel the smoke. But the domino players would pay no attention to her.

I didn't understand everything that was going on then but I knew it was bad because my father had changed. He didn't play the harmonica anymore, or tell jokes, or throw his voice.

He didn't make as much noise, and I missed it. He didn't stomp the floor when he put on his shoes the way he did in Hamlin and Stamford. He was wounded. As hard as he worked, he wasn't making a living. Hadn't even been able to buy Christmas presents for his family. I'm glad now he didn't know that things were going to get worse.

On the Road

WHEN SPRING CAME, we moved again. But not into a house. We didn't move into anything, unless you could say it was a 1922-model Chevrolet. We stored our belongings and got in that old car and lived on the road with our father for three months. We squeaked and rattled over a considerable portion of Texas while he went in and out of stores, trying to sell his package-sealing machines. We stayed in what were then called tourist camps. A few such places were already being called tourist *courts*. These were the forerunners of motels. In a tourist camp you would get a cabin for maybe a couple of bucks. It would have beds in it and little else. There would be tables outside where you could fix a meal, and you shared toilets and showers with everybody in the camp.

Going on the road that way was supposed to be an economy for us. It was explained to me that our father had to travel in order to make a living and he calculated that we could all travel with him for very little more than he spent on himself, and that way there'd be no house rent. That was the problem. We couldn't pay the rent, which was about thirty dollars a month.

Taking an entire family on the road to save money does sound strange, in these times of hundred-dollar hotel rooms and twenty-dollar steaks in restaurants. But we didn't stay in any hotels, or eat any steaks, either. In fact, if we went into a restaurant to get as much as a hamburger the entire summer I don't remember it.

The idea of traveling with our father seemed wonderful to Ima Ruthie and me. It sounded like a summer-long vacation. We had never gone on vacation anywhere, the way some people did. Nearest we ever came to a vacation trip was going to Grandma Hale's Farm for a few days.

Hitting the road didn't appeal to our mother and my sister Maifred. It puzzled me that our mother looked so sad the day the truck came to move our furniture out of the house and take it to a warehouse for storage. Even then I ought to have understood why she was sad. Here was this woman who wanted, more than anything, a decent home for her family and she was seeing her home-things being taken away. Not just furniture. Everything. Clothes. Keepsakes. Family pictures. All she'd been able to accumulate in almost twenty years of marriage. Maybe she sensed that she would never see her things again. Because she didn't.

The hope was that by the end of summer, the economy would brighten and stores would have more business and my father would sell more machines. Then we would return to Fort Worth and rent a house before school took up again.

I liked that summer on the road. But I remember my sister Maifred spent most of her time in the back seat daydreaming and writing letters and wishing she was back in Fort Worth where her friends were. Suppose you were a pretty girl of eighteen, with a year of college behind you, and you were obliged to travel all summer with your family. In a rattletrap car. To places like Monahans. Muleshoe. Cameron. Hearne.

We were all pretty good daydreamers and that helped.

I had this paint horse and a new saddle then. When the road got long I jumped on that horse and I flew. I flew along with the car, keeping just a little ahead. I would jump that paint over telephone wires and lope him across the tops of houses. People below would wave and call out to me as I passed. When I rode the horse I wore my black cowboy shirt with the shiny buttons and my sheepskin chaps. Girls lifted their arms, inviting me down. The Wilson boys recognized me and said to those standing near, "He's our personal friend. He helped us deliver papers last spring."

The best thing that really happened that summer was that Ima Ruthie found sixty-five cents under a park bench.

She was always finding things and bringing them in. Combs. Caps. Schoolbooks. Crippled birds. Kittens. I suppose she went around looking, when we would wait on our father while he worked. Sometimes he would leave us in a nice place, like a park. I saw Ima Ruthie down on her knees, reaching beneath a bench, picking things up with her right hand and popping them into her left and giving off quiet squeals and whimpers.

She was picking up nickels and dimes. They must have fallen out of the pocket of a person who had sat on that bench. My guess is sixty-five cents was more than my father made that day. Sometimes he didn't make anything, no matter how many stores he called on, and so Ima Ruthie had made a great find. I don't know what was done with it but I expect it went for groceries. Cheese and bread and lunch meat.

Or maybe a part of it bought the two yo-yos that helped us through the summer. This toy had become popular that year and Ima Ruthie and I spent long hours operating yo-yos while waiting for our father.

One day we got into a conversation with a good old country boy who talked the way Texans talk now in bad Western films. He said "mo" for "more" and "yo" for "your" and "sho" for "sure." He made a remark to Ima Ruthie that we entered into our store of private expressions, along with the bottom dresser drawer. He said:

"Let me see yo yo-yo."

Those three yo's in a row, the purity and sincerity of them, seemed worth preservation. We laughed about them in town after town. When we needed to laugh, we repeated those words. People then had a deep need to laugh. We looked everywhere for things to laugh about and often found them in unlikely places. Sometimes, more than half a century later, we resurrect that old expression as a family joke. "Let me see yo yo-yo" no longer has anything to do with a yo-yo. It can mean "Let me see your pen" or "Let me see your camera." It can mean almost anything.

There was a time of great strangeness in our lives that we call The Tourist Court. This refers not just to a place but to the events that came to pass after we quit the road the summer of '29. We needed to stop being nomads but it wasn't easy. The economy had not brightened, as we hoped. It had gotten darker.

Instead of a house, which we couldn't rent, we got into two small frame cabins of a tourist court way out on South Hemphill Street in Fort Worth. A steel mill was just across the street. This was not a high class place. Uncle Roy Oxford and Grandmother Oxford joined us there. This made seven people living in two little rooms.

That place was at the edge of the city. It was rocky. Rocks lying all around. One night we were in bed and a drunk came up and began bombarding our cabin with big rocks. I mean boulders, that would need to be thrown the way a shot-putter throws in a track meet. The rocks almost caved in the walls of the cabin. Why he did this was never explained to me.

Before this time my father had always told me that I was not to be afraid, that we lived in the sort of place where people would not be harmed. But now he wasn't saying that any longer and I went ahead and got afraid. I was afraid that drunk would come in the cabin and kill us all.

I had not yet learned that boys my own age could be harmful. At The Tourist Court I learned. When I went to George Clarke Elementary, nobody there had hurt me. I met tough boys, but if you walked around them they didn't do you any harm. But out on South Hemphill I found out that I needed to stay on guard. It wasn't safe to think that everybody you met was harmless.

What provoked him I don't know but this kid came at me with a rock in his hand about the size of a baseball. I can see him lurching toward me. I would know his eyes if I saw them again. They were gray. He didn't throw the rock. He kept it in his hand and clobbered me hard as he could just above my right eye. I can hear the rock hitting bone. *Bonk!* I thought of what the doctor said. Don't get any blows to the head.

A lump about the size of the rock ballooned above my eye. The curious thing was, it didn't go away. That ought to have suggested to somebody that something was the matter with my bones, but it didn't, not just then. When my head stopped hurting, I couldn't tell that the lick with the rock had hurt anything. It just gave me that lump, and messed up my eye somewhat and made me look a little stranger. But I didn't mind that much because I was still staying away from mirrors.

The Tourist Court must have been a torment for our mother. Here was a woman who certainly hadn't been prepared to live in such a place. She wasn't any kind of High Society person, not even in Stephenville, Texas, but she was the doctor's daughter and she had been president of the Methodist Women's Missionary Society and when she married, she was expecting a decent sort of life.

Now she was just existing, in that scruffy, tough place, with drunks that heaved boulders on the roof, and her children being attacked by mean kids, and her husband broke. Not only that, her mother, Dr. Oxford's widow, lived there as well. I know she must have been thankful Dr. Oxford was gone and didn't know these things.

My sister Maifred couldn't have been doing much grinning then, either. She rode a city bus to classes at TCU and never brought friends home because she didn't want them to know how we were living. She would say, much later, about The Tourist Court, "It was one of those times I blocked out. I didn't accept that it was happening. It was as if I were dreaming, and soon I would wake up and things would be the way they once were again."

People all over the country were becoming familiar with circumstances like these, and some much worse than ours.

Bewick Street

It was the last *of the ninth inning. The Fort Worth Cats were two runs behind the Dallas Rebels at LaGrave Field. Two out. Two on. I was at bat. I was only in the second grade but I was at bat, just the same. I was pinch hitting for Cox, the right fielder. He had pulled up lame chasing a fly. He called me to him and said, "Pardner, I'm hurt. You'll have to hit for me." I was willing but I was put on a tough spot. This was the crucial game of the season. If the Cats could pull the game out they would win the pennant and represent the Texas League in the Dixie Series. The count worked to two and two. I was looking for a curve and I got it and it hung. It hung bad, and looked the size of a pumpkin. When I hit it I could tell from the feel it would go far. It went way, way out of the park and it meant a 3-2 victory for the Cats. My teammates mobbed me at the plate. Lifted me to their shoulders. In the stands, smiling and clapping, I could see my father. And with him was the orange girl. I thought: This is the finest thing that's happened since the fire in Stamford.*

When we moved out of The Tourist Court we didn't get into a house but we got into a part of one again. It was on Bewick Street, not far from where we lived the year before when I

61

started to school. Ima Ruthie and I went back to George Clarke Elementary. The orange girl was gone. Moved away, I guess.

In the early grades, Ima Ruthie was often unhappy at school and would come home crying in the middle of the day. Which is an irony because she became a person who loved school more than anybody I ever knew. She has spent, so far, the majority of her life in a schoolhouse and is still in one now and still in love with it.

But at first she didn't like school. I didn't understand why but I knew that when Ima Ruthie cried it caused things to happen and I needed to pay attention, and I did. Sometimes when she came home they didn't send her back to school, and she would get to stay home several days. I could see a potential there, even though right then I didn't need to do anything about it because I liked school all right.

The house on Bewick Street was white frame with a porch across the front. It was not intended to be a duplex. The owners shut off certain doors and rented us some of the rooms and lived in what was left. That was being done frequently by people needing help with mortgage payments, so they wouldn't lose their homes.

I count nine people living in that house and it had just one bathroom. To get to it, we had to come through our kitchen and hustle across a back porch that stretched the breadth of the house. The porch was open to the north and I was almost an adult before I quit thinking of that porch as the coldest place on the continent. I would get acquainted with country paths to outdoor toilets ten times longer than that porch but not one of them as cold.

This was the house where Grandmother Oxford died. That front porch was where she sat and said a mesquite tree is pretty. That back porch was where she slipped and fell and broke her hip. She was seventy-two.

We went to Stephenville for her funeral. The next few years we would return to Stephenville often for funerals. For fifty years I have been telling people that we did this because our

Uncle Brinky had a combination lumberyard–undertaking
parlor there and he gave us a cut rate on coffins. My sisters
insist now that this was not the case, but I don't see how it
could fail to be.

I remember playing in the lumberyard, smelling sawdust
and the sharp cleanness of fresh-cut pine boards, and I know I
was at funerals. We never went to Stephenville, or anywhere
else that far, for anything but funerals. Why would I be at
a lumberyard, sixty miles from home, if it wasn't connected
in some way to an undertaking parlor? I can see the men of
our family standing outside the lumberyard in dark-suited
bunches, smoking and talking low the way they did at funerals. Inside the lumberyard office I can see lavender coffins
resting across new sawhorses.

Our mother always made Ima Ruthie and me go up to the
coffin at funerals and peer in at the dead person. Something
was beneficial about doing that, she said. Something to do
with accepting death. Which may have been true but I didn't
get any benefit from it because I didn't look at the corpse, not
after the first time or two. I developed a system of looking at
its necktie only, if it was a man. If it was a woman I looked at
the flower on its dress. Women in Stephenville then were always buried with flowers on their dresses. I became expert at
standing by a coffin, overflowing with respect and good con-
duct, and looking down into it without seeing anything but
the knot on a necktie. I can still do it.

When Grandmother Oxford died and I was obliged to
stand and look down at her flowers, I could smell pine boards.
I could see shiny nails in wooden bins. I could see cans of
paint on shelves. How could I not have been in a lumberyard?

It's simply not convenient for me to accept that this combination lumberyard–undertaking parlor did not exist. I have
told about it now in too many places. I have written about it
in newspapers. In bull sessions, when men talked of natural
wonders, when it came my turn to speak I told about Uncle
Brinky's wonderful business and how he sold two-by-fours
and coffins out of the same establishment. How he had a long

black hearse that was always parked, waiting for a funeral, by the side of his lumber truck.

I love the undertaking parlor being in the lumberyard and they are going to have a hard time getting to me to take it out.

The long porch across the front of the Bewick Street house is where my cousin Eugene Oxford shed his skin like a snake and walked away. He did it after a severe sunburn. He peeled all at once and left his former skin in a heap. I count that as probably the most extraordinary thing I ever saw. I longed to do it myself but I always had thick hide and didn't get sunburned deep enough for a shedding of that kind.

Except when cousin Eugene and his parents and various other relatives visited us, our family was alone in that half a house after Grandmother Oxford died. This was probably why I thought our circumstances had improved. At least we had only ourselves to feed.

Also I was happy there. I got a new pair of tennis shoes and I had the sturdy handle out of a garden hoe to use as a shinny stick and it was one of the best sticks on the street. Best of all my father began feeling better. He acquired the nearest thing he could find to some livestock. I know he wanted a milk cow but he couldn't have a cow in the Fort Worth city limits so he brought home a pair of mallard ducks. He buried an old washtub in the back yard for the ducks to swim in. They grew fat and so big they filled up the tub when they both got in it at once. Then they mated and had a great flock of babies, about a dozen, so we were in the duck business. I am not sure the neighbors were as pleased about this as my father was. When it rained, the parent ducks would lead their flock out from behind our house and parade along the sidewalk in front, flapping and quacking and being happy in the rain.

But aside from that, we stayed fairly citified on Bewick Street. I think of this chapter of our lives as the time when we began getting urbanized. My sister Maifred was back in TCU, thanks to the marvelous institution of credit. My father signed a note for her books and tuition and she would be making payments on that debt many years after she began working. My mother seemed encouraged, too. She joined the Missionary Society at Hemphill Heights Methodist Church and made new friends.

She got a new dress, and pretended she didn't want it, that we ought not to have spent the money for it. She didn't go out and buy a dress, you can bet the farm on that. My father just brought it home. She used to tell me when we were alone that one of my father's faults was in managing what money he had. She said, "Even when he gets hold of money, he doesn't know what to do with it. He won't put it into anything that'll grow to him. When he gets ten dollars, he'll go out and spend eight of it on a new dress." But there wasn't anything to be done about it, and she certainly needed the dress.

I learned a lot of city things on Bewick. To play sandlot baseball. To ride a streetcar across town and watch a professional baseball game at LaGrave Field. And to play tin-can shinny, the most citified thing of all.

You may not know the game of tin-can shinny. It's a form of field hockey. For hockey sticks we used thick poles, thick as the handle of a baseball bat. Not broomsticks, which would never stand up. That's why I had the handle out of a garden hoe for a hockey stick. It was the most valuable of my possessions. I did not own a baseball bat. When we lived in Stamford my father had gotten me one but it went into storage with everything else we owned when we traveled the summer of '29. We still talked about some day getting everything out of the warehouse but we had to pay storage costs to do that and there was no way.

In shinny, the players chose up sides and ran up and down the street trying to knock a tin can across the goal of the opposition. After that can had been knocked along the block a few times, it became compacted into a deadly missile with sharp metal points sticking out all around. When it was hit solidly, that awful thing would go spinning past the ears of the players and I am amazed that any of us ever got home to supper without serious wounds.

You can understand that tin-can shinny was a fertile source of bumps on the head, when a kid was darting about in the middle of a dozen flailing sticks. I got plenty of bumps, which according to that doctor I wasn't supposed to get, and they behaved different from the bumps of other boys. When I got a lick on a bony place it was as if the bone itself swelled up, and wouldn't go down. We didn't know it but this was symptomatic of an unusual bone disease. I would hear no name put to it for another twenty years, and it didn't much matter that nothing was done about it. There was no treatment for the condition anyhow.

The main thing that bothered me about getting those bumps was that my mother was forever staring at me when she thought I didn't know it. This made me feel like some kind of laboratory bug under study. I wanted to tell her, "Don't *look* at me!" But I didn't, for reasons I have already explained.

The Fort Worth Cats had a Knothole Gang and I became a card-carrying member along with all the other boys on our block. We would ride downtown on the streetcar and then walk on out to LaGrave Field. We sat in the right-field bleachers and we got in free. Which was fortunate because none of us had any money to spend, the way youngsters do now at ball games. I am saying we did not have even a nickel for a soda pop. There was a water fountain like we had on the schoolground and if we wanted a drink we drank from that. Just ordinary pipe-temperature water. The idea of eating something like a hotdog at a baseball game was entirely foreign to us. We didn't think about that. We were just happy to be in a real pro baseball park.

The Cats played in the Texas League which was a minor league but I did not consider it minor in any way. We knew about the New York Yankees and the Brooklyn Dodgers but they were of small significance. They could have been playing in a foreign country. They weren't in the same class with the Fort Worth Cats, the greatest baseball team in the world.

The hero of the Knothole Gang was a right fielder named Cox. He was the only player on the team who had a face. The infielders and other outfielders never got near enough to us that we could see their faces. But Cox was right out there in front of us. Sometimes he would even wave to us. When he had to drift back and pick a deep flyball off the fence, within a few feet of where we sat, we would all come near to wetting our pants it was such a thrill. If he came to bat and connected and drove a homer into our bleachers, we would be transported into frenzied rapture, world without end, amen.

One afternoon Cox looked at me. This was between innings and a stray ball had rolled to the fence in right field and he trotted after it. When he retrieved the ball, just before he threw it back toward the infield he glanced up, and for a second he looked right into my face.

That night at supper I told about that and they nodded and said, "Well, fine." But they didn't understand what it meant.

Somehow my father got hold of a portable phonograph, an old Victrola, and a few scratchy records. My guess is he traded for them. When he would make a small sale in a store sometimes he would take his commission in merchandise. The records were cowboy ballads. Within two days my sister Ima Ruthie had memorized the words to every song and could sing along perfectly with the cowboys. She had, from her beginning, an astonishing ability to memorize lyrics. She must now know the words to ten thousand songs. It's mysterious to me that a person with such a retentive memory is unable to recall Uncle Brinky's lumberyard–undertaking parlor, or the eyes of the Booger Man in Homeyers' garage.

One of the songs on the Victrola records was "When the Work's All Done This Fall." Ima Ruthie made me learn the words and sing with her. She was always making me do things like that. She persuaded me to tap dance with her, which turned out to be an unfortunate mistake. On my part, I mean. For several years afterward, when Ima Ruthie would perform I would have to perform with her.

She would perform at the slightest opportunity. When we would have company—and we had a lot of it, mostly relatives

passing through, running from Hard Times—Ima Ruthie
was called on to sing and dance. The piano was in the warehouse collecting dust and storage charges so Ima Ruthie had
to play her ukulele or the Victrola for accompaniment. Dancing and strumming the uke at the same time was no burden
for her. She could even dance and wind the Victrola without
missing a tap.

It would be several years before we got our first radio so
Ima Ruthie's act was the best in musical entertainment we
could offer to company. I think now she made me perform
with her mainly because she was afraid I'd feel left out, when
the fact was I liked being left out. I didn't enjoy audiences the
way Ima Ruthie did, but I danced and sang with her so I
wouldn't hurt her feelings.

One time Uncle Clay Oxford was stretching one of his visits with us and heard Ima Ruthie and me sing "When the
Work's All Done This Fall." That ballad is about a cowboy
who keeps saying he is going home to see his mother, that he
will go just as soon as all the work on the ranch is done in the
fall. Then when he finally gets the work done and goes to see
his mother, the dear person has gone on to glory and the
cowboy is too late. That sort of story appealed to us then.

Uncle Clay had been up in the Midwest, working in the
cornfields of Nebraska and Kansas. He said he had heard
singers who got paid, and paid well, and they were not any
better than Ima Ruthie and I. This excited and encouraged us.
At least it excited and encouraged Ima Ruthie. Years later it
occurred to me that when Uncle Clay said those singers in the
Midwest were getting paid well, he didn't specify whether
they were paid for singing or for pulling corn.

Also, when Uncle Clay visited us in those times, he wasn't
in a position to leave behind anything but complimentary re-
marks on the entertainment.

Once my mother called me in to tell him good-by. He was
a big man, with heavy shoulders and hammy hands. And
sad eyes. In the kitchen he said to my mother, "May, I hate to
ask, but could you let me have a nickel for tobacco?" Without

a word or a nod she went to her purse and dug in it and snapped open the little coin pouch in the bottom and picked out a nickel for Uncle Clay. I had respect for a nickel and yet it moved me to see this great hulking man asking for five cents, like a child who wanted candy.

We stood on the front porch and watched him plod off down the street. Everything he owned was wrapped in a newspaper and tied with a string and tucked beneath his strong arm. My mother put her hand on my shoulder and tried to give that scene value for me:

"Look at him. He doesn't even know where he'll sleep tonight, or how he'll get anything to eat. And he's got to beg a nickel to buy tobacco."

I thought of what I would do if I had that coin. I knew a little grocery store where you could buy two beautiful peanut patties for five cents, each bigger than a saucer. There were bargains then that seem impossible now. People with modest but regular incomes must have lived well indeed. Uncle Clay could get a sack of Bull Durham or Golden Grain cigarette tobacco for my mother's nickel, and the roll-your-own papers came with it. That five cents would buy two quarts of milk at certain stores, if you had the bottles to turn in. A milk price war was on. The bottles became more valuable than the milk they held. Ima Ruthie and I would go to the store and turn in two bottles and get a quart of milk, without any cash outlay. It was better than having a cow in the back yard, although my father would not have agreed.

In our school there was a boy named Edgar. He was older, as we said. That meant he was not the same age as the students in his grade. Edgar was probably in the fifth grade, and ought to have been in the seventh. He was head and shoulders larger than his classmates. These were times when teachers flunked children if they couldn't do their schoolwork.

So this Edgar was a flunker but his age made him just about the most effective teacher in that school. He lectured in secret places, and we listened and believed everything.

He first got my attention by taking a piece of chalk out of his pocket and writing FUCK on the wall of the boys' restroom. Then he gave a talk on the meaning of the word, and its significance in the world. If we had listened to our teachers in class the way we listened to Edgar, we would all have been straight-A students. He was an encyclopedia of information, and all of it wrong. Or simply untrue.

In his lectures he would tell us how he had coaxed this girl or that one into the weeds over by the railroad tracks on the way home. Then he had laid them down and taken off their underwear and put it to them, as he liked to say, and it made them howl. He always made them howl.

These would be the prettiest girls in school and when I saw them in the halls I could not escape the images of Edgar's lectures. I would see these nice girls in the weeds, writhing and howling. And hurting, I supposed, or else why would they howl?

Despite what Edgar probably thought, he did not introduce me to all the world's biological wonders. A kid doesn't spend his summers on a farm without finding out about procreation. Creatures in the country are mating constantly, or they've just gotten through, or they're about to begin. Roosters chasing hens. Bulls mounting cows. Dogs locked together in mysterious ways in the yard. Tomcats "fighting" with tabbycats. Some mornings you could walk out of Grandma Hale's back door and every living thing you could see was screwing, with the exception of the people.

So early along it was explained to me—certainly not by my parents, however—that when your father put it to your mother it produced *you*. I did have some trouble with that. I accepted that cows and bulls did it to make calves but one thing I knew for sure: *My* parents didn't do it that way. Other mothers and fathers might, but not mine. Well, at least not my mother. She was a Methodist, don't forget. She wouldn't do such a thing. I kept that opinion to myself, though. If I had expressed it to the older boys they would have said,

"Where did you come from then? You think they found you in a holler stump?"

But Edgar in the restroom did have a considerable influence on my view of biology. If you had to make them howl, as he said, I wasn't much interested. Why would I want to make a girl howl?

Also I refuted Edgar's claim that when babies were born, they came out from between their mother's legs, right here, see. I put that aside because it made me uncomfortable. By then I had seen calves emerge from their mothers and I had watched eight kittens get born in a box behind the cookstove. But I held out for a better system on human babies.

The trouble was, I kept going back to that packing crate in Stamford. "There it is," she said. Yes, but no baby could come out of a place like that, even if it got four times bigger than it was in 1928. If one did, it would have to hurt something awesome. Then when I found out that it did in fact hurt, my position in this matter was cemented and I still think to this time that having babies that way is messy and unfair. But I have learned to stay quiet about it because people keep asking me to suggest alternate ways.

About this time, in addition to sex lectures illustrated on restroom walls, I was introduced to serious religion.

We had always gone to church with fierce loyalty because of our mother. She seemed to think of us as a solid Methodist family who weren't as downtrodden financially as we really were. True, we showed up for church looking a great deal less than prosperous and sometimes we might have looked downright shabby but that was only because we didn't want to seem proud. At least that's how I think our mother felt about it. Pride was one of the principal sins, wasn't that right?

We had the contradiction that, at home, being religious embarrassed us. It certainly embarrassed me, when practiced openly, and I think it did my father as well. For instance, we couldn't pray out loud. We couldn't say blessings before meals as so many other families did. I knew Baptist kids who talked about something called "family Bible reading" and sessions around the fire at night when each person would "lead in prayer." I soon learned what leading in prayer meant. It meant you had to pray out loud, so that everybody could hear you talking to God. It was too much like public confession to suit me. I couldn't handle that.

Say I found a cap pistol, and I knew whose it was but pretended I did not. Say I hid it away until it was forgotten, so I could bring it out after a long time and have it for myself. Do you suppose I would want to confess that crime in public? Certainly not. (Never mind where I got that example.)

But I could make the confession in private. I could send it up after dark, twisting and whistling, rising through the ceiling and the roof and the hackberry leaves and the clouds. But I surely wasn't about to do it when we were all sitting around in a ring, keeping count of who did what.

One time when we had gone to Grandma Hale's Farm, the entire gang attended a Sunday dinner at Aunt Nellie Minnick's. Aunt Nellie was my father's sister and lived not far from Grandma's. Before we ate, somebody called on my father to say the blessing and he refused. I was proud of him for that. I imagined it meant he hated praying in public, as I did. I wished I could talk to him about it but that was not possible.

On Easter Sunday in 1930 I was taken into the membership of the Methodist Church. They asked me if I would accept Jesus Christ as my personal savior and I said I would. I said it because my mother told me to. I believed Jesus Christ was the son of God because my mother said he was and she had never been known to tell a lie.

I joined the church along with a great gang of other children. I didn't need to be baptized because of the sprinkling I'd had back in Stephenville. It wasn't enough water for the Baptists but it was plenty for the Methodists.

My mother had talked to me a lot about joining the church. I suspect she sensed that I wasn't as enthusiastic about it as I ought to have been. She talked to me about The Devil. She said when I was reluctant to do what I knew was right, that was The Devil working on me. She said when I told a fib, The Devil was the cause. If I went to bed without doing my homework or saying my prayers, it meant The Devil had got hold of me.

She spoke with dread in her voice and yet I found a vague comfort in what she said. If it was The Devil who made me find the cap pistol and not return it where it belonged, maybe the sin was his and not mine. I knew that was a weak position but I needed comfort and took it from any source.

My mother said The Devil appeared in many forms. She said he did not wear a red suit. He did not have a long tail with a stinger on the end. She said he could be a handsome man in a double-breasted suit who might come up and tell me it was all right to smoke cigarettes. She said he could even be a woman.

This was powerful stuff. I wondered if The Devil could be in Charlotte, a girl older than I was. She lived on our block and when she smiled at me I felt the heat in my face and I wanted to look up her dress. But I did not mention this to my mother.

I fell into the habit of watching for The Devil. Since he came in so many disguises I supposed he needed to be watched for on a steady basis. I never watched for God because I already knew what he looked like. He looked like the North Wind.

In Miss Green's first-grade class there had been a picture book with a story about the North Wind. It was illustrated by a drawing, a great round male face in the sky. It was made all of clouds. Beard of clouds. Hair of clouds. Eyes and mouth of clouds. Great puffy cheeks of clouds, and all white. For me it was the face of God. Also of Santa Claus. The face of God and Santa Claus in the sky.

My mother talked to me often about my soul. She said the only part of me that couldn't die was my soul, that when I died my body would be buried but my soul would rise up to heaven and last forever. My soul, then, was my most important part, a thing I couldn't even see. I thought it ought to be seen, so I began seeing it and it was in the shape of a football, and about the color of a new saddle.

I can't say why it was shaped that way except that it seemed to fit my body. It was positioned inside me and extended from the bottom of my neck down just below my bellybutton. I figured out that everyone's soul was that way, and when they died their souls rose out of them and went in slow motion up to heaven, traveling end over end. I was able to see this happening. It was obvious to me that anybody could have seen souls rising at the funerals they attended but they were too busy crying and carrying on and never bothered to watch.

At funerals I attend now the undertakers try to spare the survivors as much torment as possible but in my early times it was the other way around. Funeral customs then wanted tears and sobs and the more the better.

Consider the graveside service. Its stated purpose was to comfort the family. The preacher would even smile, and read a happy poem, and tell us not to weep because our loved one was going to be with Jesus. Fine. That was good to hear, and gradually the comfort began to take effect. The sobs got quieter, and then stopped. You could hear the wind swishing through the cedars and the mesquites. Maybe you'd hear a subdued sniffle, an occasional nose getting blown. Signs of recovery.

And then:

I wish I may never again see a sunset if the undertaker didn't pick that moment to start cranking the coffin down into the ground. And a church quartet would grope its way into a nasal rendition of "Nearer My God to Thee" and here would come the sobs and the whoops again from the mourners.

On about the third stanza of the singing and the wailing, the grave fillers would begin shoveling dirt onto the lowered coffin. All our folks were buried in arid ground. The first shovelfuls that went back into the grave were clods of clay the size of grapefruit. They would thud and break when they hit the coffin and you'd get this scratching, rolling sound that was made by the pieces of dry clod that had broken on impact. It was an awful sound and it inspired the mourners to new heights of lamentation.

At Maimie's funeral, when we were all walking away from the grave at last, holding onto each other, red-eyed and sniffly, I turned around and looked and saw my grandmother's soul, escaping from the grave. There it went, rising in slow motion, end over end, ascending into heaven, getting out of that awful hole in the ground. It was a pretty thing to watch and it pleased me that I was able to see it. Nobody else saw it. They didn't even turn around to look.

Souls rising that way was a part of our religion that I liked.

I joined the church in my brown corduroy knickers and my black and white tennis shoes. A boy named Ted who was in my class at school joined along with me. The next morning when we were standing in line on the schoolground, waiting to march in, he asked me if I felt any different now that I had joined the church. I told him no. "Me neither," he said, and seemed relieved.

But my mother felt different. She was pleased, and so I was glad I joined.

Glen Rose

GLEN ROSE is about sixty miles southwest of Fort Worth on the Paluxy, a pretty rock-bottomed stream that never has decided whether to be a creek or a river. In most of its places and times it's a creek but when heavy rains come to its watershed, it can get to be an adult river in a hurry. The stream goes through the middle of the town, which was home to maybe 1,500 souls when we moved there.

For a country town, Glen Rose was pretty widely known for three reasons. One, it had a great underground supply of evil-smelling, god-awful-tasting water that spurted up from artesian wells. My father said the water came from the bowels of the earth, and had the flavor to prove it.

Texas in these times was in love with strange waters containing sulfur and salts. Somebody was always starting resorts in places where this water squirted or bubbled out of the ground. People with rheumatism and stomach trouble came and bathed in the stuff. At Glen Rose, some drank it and testified to its curative powers. My father said the principal effect of the water was to make you go to the bathroom six times a day. Whatever its effect was, Glen Rose was a health resort and had sanitariums along the banks of the Paluxy.

Which was lucky for the Hales because it gave us a story to tell about why we moved out of the city. We did it because of our mother's health. I told that story for years and never knew its source. The source might even have been me.

"Why did you move to Glen Rose?"

"It's a health resort, and our mother was sick."

She wasn't sick. She was probably the healthiest individual in the clan. It was her job to take *care* of the sick, not to *be* sick. She stayed well for seventy years and when the time came, she got sick and went to bed and died in a month. But she wasn't sick when we went to Glen Rose, except maybe in her heart.

Because we were going backward instead of forward in the matter of finances and living standards, and her piano and her cookstove and her living-room davenport were gone forever.

The second thing Glen Rose was known for, it was the seat of government for Somervell County, which was the source of the best moonshine whiskey in the Southwest. I would bet you a paint horse my mother didn't know that when we moved there or she wouldn't have gone.

The third thing was that back in Cretaceous time, dinosaurs walked along the Paluxy. These great reptiles left footprints in the mud which hardened into Somervell County's present rocks and this gave the area several sets of dinosaur tracks. Tourists come there now to see where dinosaurs walked.

The leadership of that region in recent times caused one dinosaur track to be lifted out of solid rock and built into the wall of a bandstand on the courthouse square. Which I thought was a mistake but never mind that. Then the government of Texas created a state park at Glen Rose with life-sized dinosaurs done in plastic, or plaster, or whatever. I class that a greater mistake than the county made but I will move along and try to keep to the subject.

The real reason we moved to Glen Rose was that we located there a cheaper place to hide from Hard Times. We lived in another half of a house, with lower rent than the half of a house in Fort Worth. It was owned by a Mrs. Nichols, a widow with white hair.

She had been living alone in that house, which had a large sleeping porch across one side. My father made a deal. We would get the living room and the porch, where we all slept, and Mrs. Nichols would keep to her side of the house except for the kitchen. We would both use the kitchen on a take-turns basis. Mrs. Nichols would cook and eat and get out and then we would go in and cook and eat.

So in Glen Rose we didn't share a bathroom as in Fort Worth but we did share a kitchen. The reason we didn't share a bathroom is that there wasn't one. We bathed in washtubs in the kitchen after supper, when we were fairly certain Mrs. Nichols wouldn't come in.

Whatever citification we had picked up in Fort Worth we lost quickly in Glen Rose. Our mother went back to cooking on a wood-burning stove, when in Fort Worth she had already moved up to natural gas. To go to the toilet, we waltzed down a rocky path to the privy. Mrs. Nichols' house had no running water. A few steps from the back door there was a shallow well with a little short-handled pitcher pump. The water it brought up was cool and clear and had none of the rotten-egg taste of the mineral water that made Glen Rose famous.

I came to love that little pump. I liked the way it rattled and squeaked and gurgled. When I would roam in hot weather through the cedar brakes and get thirsty, it pleased me to visualize that little pump in the back yard, waiting to welcome me with its noises and its cool water. It was a friendly pump. I suppose to my parents and to my sister Maifred that pump represented a retreat into poverty, but it didn't to me.

When I was tracing the path of our flight from Hard Times, getting ready to do this book, I returned to Glen Rose and found Mrs. Nichols' house. The old sleeping porch has been removed and the house renovated and painted and it looks fine. The yard is covered in a heavy sod of St. Augustine grass which seems curious because when we lived there the yard was just dirt, and rocks, and scattered patches of native grass and weeds. We lived often in rocky places. The Nichols place was a country house at the edge of the town. Across the red sandy road from our front gate was a pasture where cattle grazed.

I knocked on the door and told the lady who answered that I thought I had lived in her house at one time, long ago, and it was very important to me to know whether I had the right house. One way I could tell. The house used to have a pitcher pump in the back yard and some trace of the well might remain.

"Never was a pump in the yard of *this* house," she said.

But would she mind if I looked?

"Go ahead." She shrugged, and walked through and met me in the back yard, which was heavily sodded the same as the front. I walked straight to the place. I hadn't been there in fifty years but I knew the spot exactly. I knew how many steps to take from the back door before I reached out to grab the pump handle.

With my fingers I dug into the grass and spread it and sunlight glinted off a metal disk where the well had been capped and the pump removed. The woman was certainly surprised.

Finding that cap made me feel really good, for a reason I'm not sure anyone else can understand or appreciate. It wasn't because I was able to show the woman a small thing in her yard she didn't know was there. It had to do with my friendship with that pump. I looked on that pump as one of the goodnesses of my life, the way it would respond to a few strokes of its handle by producing that sweet water on a hot day. The metal cap, buried in the grass, is like a historical marker to that bizarre time of our lives. To me it whispers, "Yes, you were here."

I had good times in Glen Rose. Ima Ruthie and I went to school only half a term and I don't believe I learned anything in that old red brick schoolhouse. But outside of it I learned a very great deal.

I caught my first fish in the Paluxy, and learned to swim in one of its pools. I learned to kill wild creatures and to like the feeling it gave me. I learned to play hooky from school. I learned how to endure hours and hours of sitting in church services. I even learned what a whiskey still looks like. Furthermore, in Glen Rose my father talked to me about sex, or anyway he came close, and he told me a dirty joke for the first time, and almost for the last. I also learned how desperately a person can love a dog, and how it hurts to lose one. I finished learning to cuss, too. In Fort Worth I had gotten a fair foundation but that was mainly urban cussing. Glen Rose profanity was country, and much more earthy, richer, and satisfying. Therefore I suffered withering guilt pains from doing it. But all the boys I ran with were cussers and so I had no choice.

Along with my cousins George and Riley Oxford I wandered the cedar brakes along the Paluxy. We said we were hunting for whiskey stills, and sometimes we came across one but it would always be abandoned. We fell in with older boys who knew how to play hooky and tell lies at home about what happened in school that day. We tried to do everything the older boys did but it was hard.

It was the custom among boys to declare their defiance of authority by going to remote places and shouting forbidden words. The Paluxy had wonderful high rocky bluffs. You could stand on their rocky rims and look across the river at the town. We seemed a thousand feet high. We might have been two hundred. We would be within sight of the courthouse, the school, the churches, our own homes, but far out of hearing range. It was counted courageous to cup hands at the mouth and lift the voice high and spell out the worst of all words:

"Ef-f-f-f-f! Few-w-w-w-w! See-e-e-e-e! Kay-y-y-y-y!"
Or:
"Es-s-s-s-s! Say-y-y-y-y! Chigh-h-h-h-h! Tee-e-e-e-e!"

After a performance we would all be quiet a few seconds, while the echoes traveled along the river.

I was not able to enjoy cussing as much as the others because I was already a member of the Methodist Church and therefore not entitled to take part. I would take part anyhow but when I got the chance I would duck behind a cedar bush and ask forgiveness. It had been explained to me that you could go to hell for cussing and there wasn't any way, any place that you could go and cuss without God hearing you. Before I joined the church I imagined that I could pull the covers over my head and say an ugly word, or crawl under the house, and not even God could hear me. But then my mother told me I couldn't even have a thought that God wouldn't know about. I admired a God with that kind of capability but it seemed an invasion of my privacy that I wasn't able to have even a thought for myself and nobody else.

It was common then for parents and Sunday School teachers to talk to children about the torture of hell. I found out at Hemphill Heights Methodist Church what the Devil did to you if you went to hell. He pitched you naked into a pit of red-hot coals and you stayed there forever. You burned, but you weren't allowed to burn all the way up. You couldn't die and get the hurting over with because you were already dead. It was a dreadful idea.

One time I was helping my mother wash and I got a demonstration of what hell would be like. This was when people washed country-style, by boiling clothes in a washpot outdoors. I was barefooted, and stepped in some ashes near the fire. The ashes happened to be covering a solid bed of live coals. These produce a special sort of pain.

First comes a kind of sticking sensation on the bottom of the foot, as if you have stepped on a grass bur. Then the pain spreads, gradually, across the sole of the foot and you think, well, it's bad, yes, but it's just about over and I can stand it. But it's *not* over. It slowly gets worse, and keeps getting worse, and you imagine that it will never reach its peak. And when it does, you finally discover what unbearable pain is, for a few seconds.

A few seconds. And you think, that's what the coals of hell are like, except they'll be burning you not just a few seconds but forever and ever. And not just on the bottom of your foot but all over your naked self.

This was the reason I couldn't stand on the bluff and shout ef-few-see-kay without running into the brush and asking God to forgive me. And I wasn't entirely sure I would get forgiven when I asked. There was always that doubt.

Being a member of the church was no easy path. I confess I envied the other boys who hadn't joined. They could yell any word, and laugh, and feel comfortable.

I envied my cousin George Oxford for another reason. He could pick up handfuls—no, armloads—of spiders and let them crawl all over his body and this was sometimes worth money. I wanted to do that but I could not.

Across the centuries, waters of the Paluxy dug shallow caves along the stream. Roofs and floors of these caves are often solid rock. A typical cave might be two feet from floor to ceiling, just a horizontal crevice extending back in the rock ten or twelve feet. It's common for tens of thousands of daddy longlegs spiders to congregate in such a cave. The ceiling might be a living blanket of spiders, all intertwined, dark and quivering.

Cousin George would lie on his side and scooch back into a cave and bring forth literal armloads of those long-legged spiders. He would stand grinning while they crawled over him. Over his face and ears and up and down his legs. It was a magnificent sight.

When we were on the river, tourists would sometimes come along, looking back into the caves, exclaiming at the spiders, wading in the shallows, searching for dinosaur tracks. That's when George would go get a fresh load of spiders. The tourists were astonished to meet a boy covered in spiders that way. They would want pictures, and for a nickel George would go back in a cave for more spiders and pose.

It was a profitable enterprise but I simply couldn't do it. Daddy longlegs spiders are harmless but I couldn't bear to feel them walking across my flesh. Oh, I didn't mind two or three but to make any money you had to have hundreds on you at once. You had to have at least a dozen on your face, and one or two at each ear. Cousin George became a building contractor when he grew up. I always think of him as having got his start as the Spider Boy of the Paluxy.

With the Spider Boy and his brother Riley and several other friends I learned to kill things. Wild things. Birds. Frogs. Lizards. Snakes. We killed with what is now called a slingshot. We called it by a different name that I can no longer use comfortably. The weapon was made from strips of rubber cut out of inner tubes and tied to the ends of a forked stick. Ammunition was a small rock which fit into a pocket secured to the ends of the rubber strips. The pocket was made of the leather tongue from an old shoe. Even thick and respected dictionaries now list such a weapon as a slingshot. A slingshot to us was an entirely different proposition and practically impossible to hit anything with.

Evidently it was bred into us to kill. When we went along in the woods or beside a stream or across a prairie, if we saw a wild thing we tried to kill it. No snake was a good snake. It needed to be dead, and we killed it and felt important and powerful and victorious.

This killing intellect was not just in boys. It existed even in gentle and otherwise intelligent adults, and does still. It was in my father. Our cats out there at Hamlin didn't really need prairie dog meat but pretending they did provided an excuse to shoot the animals for sport. One of my oldest memories has me riding the mare behind my father on Grandma Hale's Farm while he killed things, shooting off the horse. Not meat that we needed. Anything. Skunks. Jackrabbits. Birds. There it goes, kill it, shoot. Good shot.

Nobody questioned the sense of all that killing. If anybody had, we could have offered justification. Skunks could get in the chickenhouse and kill pullets. Hawks could swoop down and carry off a full-grown hen. (Yes, but I never saw one do it, not in all the years I spent in the country. The hawks I watched on the attack seemed to be after field mice or cotton-tail rabbits.) Then snakes. Even a snake harmless to humans could do damage. Take a chicken snake. It could eat eggs as fast as the hens could lay. Jackrabbits, well, they could do damage in the garden. And lizards. I forget what damage we had thought up for a little striped lizard to do. But a lizard was generally the first creature a country boy killed.

I suppose we could have said that we needed to kill lizards for practice, so we could later move on with ease to bigger animals that stole food from our mouths. But we didn't say any such thing. We didn't say anything at all. We just killed. Boys, especially. It was one of the principal differences between boys and girls. Girls sat on the porch and played jacks. Boys went out and killed things.

I would reach a time when all this killing of wild creatures came back to torture my conscience and change me into a dedicated non-killer.

Glen Rose was where my father's work died. He wasn't fired. His job just played out. Business across Texas was so bad that few store owners would buy package-sealing machines. My father continued to get letters from the company but he seldom went out to sell. I learned the reason was that the company would not advance him expense money and he simply didn't have enough to buy gas to get out of town. A time or two he went out with another traveling salesman who let him ride along. He would come home looking sleepless and tired and just flat hungry. Nobody asked him how he had done on the trip. It was written on his face.

It was strange, having him home during the day. We weren't used to him being home. He would do woman-things. Help our mother cook. Scrub clothes with her. Shell peas. Wash dishes.

But it wasn't as if those two stayed in a state of dejection. In fact, many days they seemed to have fun working together in that unaccustomed way. We would hear them laughing, or singing, and that was reassuring. I felt that as long as they could laugh and sing, things couldn't be so bad.

Furthermore, I began to get time with my father that I'd never had before. Afternoons he would come out and knock flyballs to me. There was nothing I loved more. I believe if he had stayed out eight solid hours and swung the bat, I would never have tired of it.

We even went fishing together on the Paluxy. A rare treat for me, fishing with my father. We dug worms together. Walked to the river. Rigged perch and catfish lines on poles cut from willows. We actually talked. Visited. He would tell stories of places he'd been, people he'd known on the road. I would ask questions and he would answer them in the most interesting style. Conversation with my father. It was wonderful.

One afternoon we sat together on the riverbank, waiting for the catfish to bite, and he brought up the subject of sex. He had never given me the customary birds-and-bees talk and I suppose he figured it was about time he got it over with.

I knew a little way in advance that he was sneaking up on the subject because he called attention to a cow and a bull just across the river. I had already noticed them. The cow was obviously in heat. The bull was following along just behind her, and sometimes he would stand close with his ear touching her side. My considerable experience at observing sex among domestic animals told me the bull had already put it to her at least once and was very likely about to do so again pretty soon. I had lived most of my time with milk cows in the back yard and I knew the basic moves in dairy cattle breeding.

My father said, "See that bull over yonder, and the cow?"
I said I did.
"Well," he said, "you watch."
I could see his tack. He knew I'd seen cattle breed but I guess he wasn't certain I was familiar with the human equivalent and intended to strike a parallel.

Then the bull did an ordinary thing that bulls everywhere

do. He sniffed at the cow in a very private place. Next he turned toward the river, lifted his head, and wrinkled his nose in a spectacular way, as if showing distaste.

I heard a quiet laugh from my father, muffled, as if he didn't intend for it to escape.

He said suddenly, "You know why a bull will wrinkle his nose and make a face that way every time he sniffs under a cow's tail?"

"No, why?"

"Because he wants all the other bulls to think it smells bad."

Well. It was an old joke even then but I hadn't heard it and I laughed. Tentatively, at first, because I wasn't certain if I was supposed to. I understood the joke well enough but I couldn't believe I was hearing it told to me by my own father. I'm still not certain that it didn't just pop out of him, unplanned.

I didn't want to look at him. I kept my eye on the river. But I could hear him giving off grunts of near-silent laughter and I couldn't hold it any longer—I exploded. And so did he just afterward, and presently we were both holding our stomachs and rolling on the riverbank in a laughing fit, all out of control. The bullfrogs and the water moccasins and the herons and cranes must have wondered at the racket, not common on rivers. Laughter, going upstream and down, bouncing off rocks, echoing among the cottonwoods and willows.

Every few seconds we would try to recover and stop but then we'd look at each other and when I saw his face and the tears coursing from beneath his glasses I would re-explode, and so would he, and there we'd go for another round.

Toward the end, when we almost had it under control, we had sat up, and were wiping our eyes. We looked across the river and the bull and the cow had chosen that instant to perform the act I was intended to witness. That launched us again. I can't quite explain all that laughter. I suppose it was a release, for both of us, from an awkward moment. But our laughter was also, I think, a celebration of gladness, marking the time the barrier between man and boy came down and we could share something private that we wouldn't talk about to women or girls.

We didn't catch a fish. Don't think we even got a nibble. But that was by far the best fishing trip I was ever on. When the laughing stopped and the bull and the cow went on down the river, we took up our lines and left.

He said not one further word to me about sex, that day or any other.

But we were changed, walking home. We were different from when we dug the worms and started out. I felt closer to him. I felt taller, too. I stretched my legs, and walked in step with him.

It's a mystery to me what we used for money to pay the rent and buy groceries those months in Glen Rose. The stop in that place marked one of our low spots, economically. A little later on we would hit a couple of lower ones but Glen Rose was low. And yet, I felt a curious happiness there that has stayed with me.

Our mother evidently finished her time of grieving over the death of her own mother and she began to have a little fun, it seemed to me. She could be rigid about religion and morals but she was a good sport about clean fun. She would go to the river with us sometimes, and wade all day in the shallows, and carry peanut butter sandwiches for a picnic lunch. We would take old towsacks, their seams opened with a razor blade, and she would help us stitch the burlap together to make crude seines and we'd seine for small fish in the Paluxy. I remember the pleasure she got one day when we found a big dinosaur track at the edge of the stream and it was full of water and we put into it the fish we seined. She liked telling about that, for years afterward, how we kept the little fish we caught in a flooded dinosaur track.

She was always happy when we went to church and I guarantee you we had plenty of church-going in Glen Rose. Aunt Addie Lee Autry and her husband Uncle Cleveland Autry came to live near us. Uncle Cleveland was a preacher. A preacher without a church. He decided to have a revival and convert a few folks in Somervell County.

The only thing I liked about that revival was that it made my mother happy. She announced we would attend every service. They were held at night, outdoors, on a vacant lot on the square across the street from the courthouse.

It sure got tedious. Every night after supper we would all trudge downtown to the revival meeting. We didn't really go every night for two solid months. It only seemed like two months. Those services were a great embarrassment to me. Uncle Cleveland's preaching embarrassed me, and Aunt Addie Lee's arm-twisting did too.

What I mean by arm-twisting, she would go out into the congregation during the service and scout for prospects. She would ask them if they were saved or not and if they admitted they weren't, she would put the pressure on them to go forward and meet Uncle Cleveland in front of the pulpit and accept Jesus.

Aunt Addie Lee was a very large woman. I have always thought of her as a loomer. No matter how big a sinner she got hold of out there in the audience, still she loomed over him. If I had not already been a member of the church I would have gone up front and joined in a split minute, just to get Aunt Addie Lee to quit looming over me.

While she was out in the audience prospecting for lost sheep, Uncle Cleveland would be in front of the crowd, crying. That was a further embarrassment. In those times among country preachers we had a variety of styles. We had a lot of shouters. We had moaners and groaners. We had mutterers and stutterers. We had whisperers and gaspers. Then we had criers. Uncle Cleveland was a crier. I could see it showed a considerable talent, preaching and crying both at once, and the first night I admired it. The second night I didn't admire it as much as the first. By the end of the third night I was out of admiration entirely, and began just to tolerate. I asked my mother why Uncle Cleveland cried so much. She always had an answer that would shut you up. She said he cried for joy, because he knew that when he died he was going to heaven and live forever in a paradise. You couldn't top my mother for answers to religious questions.

I got permission to sit on the back row, where I hoped nobody would find out I was kin to Aunt Addie Lee. Back there I saw that Uncle Cleveland's revival was heavily attended by june bugs. They were drawn to the dim electric bulbs strung temporarily over the vacant lot. A june bug falls in love with every light he sees and will try to send himself into paradise by flying straight into it at full throttle.

A bald-headed man sat with his wife in the same place every night, toward the rear of the congregation. His head was round as a cue ball and it glistened and seemed to give off as much light as one of the bulbs. Every now and then a june bug would mistake it for a light and dive for it and bounce off. That by itself was an entertainment but the admirable thing was, that old gent would never flinch when a bug hit him. That was marvelous to me. For an insect, a june bug has considerable heft. He won't bite you or hurt you but he's startling. He's got impact. I never saw a person take a direct june bug hit up the side of the head without jumping or ducking or flailing at the air or producing a mild cuss word. But this bald gent was immune. June bugs could bomb him from the opening prayer to the closing hymn and he would never twitch.

Those bugs became important to me. They helped me get through that eternal revival. I studied them. I reached a place where I could predict within two or three hits how many times june bugs would pop that gent in one night. I learned from that flock of bugs on the Somervell County Courthouse Square that I could endure the years and years of church meetings I knew were coming to me. All I had to do was to look around me, and some worthwhile diversion would pop up.

You understand that attending Uncle Cleveland's revival was in addition to regular church. Regular church was at Glen Rose Methodist. Every time one of its doors flew open, we would all be there waiting to file in.

My sister Ima Ruthie's reputation as a performer was enlarged significantly in that church. She was always getting up and singing solos. They didn't even have to give her any warning. If they wanted a solo sung, all they had to do was mention her name and she would sing it. I have known the preacher to stop in the square-center of a sermon and ask Ima Ruthie to get up and sing and she would smile and rise and go to warbling as if singing in midsermon was what the Lord set her on this earth to do.

Sometimes she would make me sing with her. I didn't like to do it because Ima Ruthie's performances were so often impromptu. If I sang with her, I wanted advance warning and the more the better. I needed to worry. I needed to work myself up into a state of nervous agitation. I needed to anticipate disaster. I needed to imagine that I would reach for a note and miss it by a yard and the audience would laugh, just the way the class laughed at me when I was trying to count by threes in Miss Hettie Green's first-grade room. Ima Ruthie needed no advance worry time.

One Sunday night the preacher had run too long to suit me so I had gone on to bed. That is, I stretched out on a pew and went to sleep. This could be gotten away with on Sunday nights when attendance was spare and plenty of unoccupied pew space was available. Pew-sleeping is some of the best you'll ever get. A bench hard as concrete. Without even a thin pillow. But it's fine sleeping because you aren't supposed to be doing it.

Ima Ruthie shook me awake and said, "Come on, we've got to sing."

I asked when and she said, "Right now. They're waiting for us. Come on."

If I ever make a list of the ten strangest experiences of my life, this will be near the top: Being awakened on a church pew and then, within twenty seconds, standing before an audience singing a duet with my sister.

Sure, I remember what we sang. The old hymn "Living For Jesus." I know why Ima Ruthie picked that one. It was because she loved to sing harmony on the chorus, and that's why she woke me. She had to have somebody to sing the tune. One thing she could never do is harmonize with herself, although I can't help being a little surprised she didn't figure out a way to do it.

Toward the end of our stay at Glen Rose, my father took me along one afternoon to the little town of Walnut Springs, a few miles south of Glen Rose in Bosque County. I noticed there a kind of arbor, with a pulpit and some wooden benches. I remarked that a revival was being held in Walnut Springs, just as Uncle Cleveland's had been held in Glen Rose.

He said, "Yeah. Well, let's not mention it to Mama, all right?"

I loved that because it was another display of our new relationship. Secrets from the women. Also it indicated that he, too, had gotten an overdose of church. We could see ourselves driving every night down to Walnut Springs if my mother learned a revival was going on there.

This was the summer I almost owned a dog. He lived across the road from us. His name was Red Dog and he was an Irish setter. He grew up in the months we spent in Somervell County.

Red Dog was what we called "subject to papers." That meant he was purebred and could have been registered with a breed association if anybody had cared to take the trouble or spend the fee to get it done. A lot of domestic animals then were said to be subject to papers, even when they weren't subject to any such thing. It was a way of bragging on a dog or a bull. Or on anything, including inanimate objects. I remember Uncle Barney Hale telling my mother her cornbread was so good it was subject to papers.

It was a shock to me to find out how much a person can love a dog. I had read stories about boys loving dogs and dogs loving boys but I didn't pay much attention. The stories seemed cornball. I just didn't yet understand about dogs.

Red Dog was a loose-jointed awkward pup when he staggered across the road from Mr. Williams' house and took my hand in his mouth. Mr. Williams was gone most every day so this setter got in the habit of staying at our house. When his range increased, he began following me. Everywhere I went that dog went along and I liked it. He became an extension of myself.

When we went to the river or roamed the cedar brakes, he was there. He loped great circles around me. He sniffed and wagged. He explored thickets and fencerows and all the holes in the ground. Now and then he would report to me, in the center of the circle he was making. He would lick my fingers and look up and say, "Don't worry. I'm on the job. Everything's under control."

He wasn't trained as a hunter. He wasn't trained as an anything. He just wanted us to be together. I'd never before had such a compliment paid me. Red Dog thought I was wonderful, just by being alive. When I went out early in the morning to wash my face at the little pump, there he was, his mouth open in a great smile. He would tell me, "Thank you for being my friend, for coming out this way and rubbing my head." If I woke up in the night, I could hear him snuffling and rustling under the house, where he slept just beneath my bed. He waited for me while I went to school. He waited for me at church. Everywhere I went. If he wasn't there when I came out, I felt diminished, incomplete. We became a part of one another.

Which was a problem, since he wasn't my dog.

When we were gathering our stuff to leave Glen Rose, Mr. Williams came and talked to my mother and father. He said that seeing the dog and I had become such friends, and the dog probably would never make much of a hunter, not now, why didn't we just take him along, wherever we were going. My father said we would think about it, see if we could figure a way to take the dog.

We didn't take him.

My best friend, who had been given to me, and we didn't take him.

I think I would not have been so nearly destroyed if I had

understood how desperate our family circumstance was at that time. There was no income. My father couldn't pay even the paltry rent Mrs. Nichols charged. We had to get out. Winter was coming, and my father was concerned about feeding us. We didn't need any additional mouths to fill. Not even a dog's.

The Farm

WE WERE *on Grandma Hale's Farm, far back in the pasture. We were looking for a lost cow named Birdie. She was due to find a calf, as the men said when the women were listening. It was not polite in mixed company to say that a cow* had *a calf, so they said that she* found *one. It sounded as if she went searching here and there and finally discovered a calf behind a bush and claimed it and brought it home. My father was with us. Also Uncle John Campbell, who was operating Grandma's Farm. We were horseback. I was riding the paint horse I had the summer of '29 when I traveled with the family, the same one I flew on, above houses and telephone poles. We heard a woman scream nearby. "It's a panther," Uncle John said. He knew about panthers. We rode to the sound and the panther, a huge thing, was slipping up on Birdie and her new calf. We yelled at it. It wheeled and charged us. My father was on the sorrel mare. The mare bolted and threw him. He lay sprawled directly in the path of the charging panther. Riding full speed, I drew my rifle from its scabbard and got two shots off and they found their mark exactly. When the panther fell, one of its great paws was within an inch of my father's arm. And so I was a hero again. They talked of this everywhere, how the boy had killed the panther and saved the life of his father.*

If any panthers were still in that part of Texas then, they might have been hunted down and killed and eaten. When we moved to Grandma Hale's Farm, country people were mighty short on meat. The Great Depression had settled in and was running deep. Jokes were made in the cities about East Texans living on armadillos and West Texans on possums. But the country folks weren't laughing at such jokes. If we saw a squirrel it was an event. Rabbits were still fairly plentiful but I went on night hunts when the dogs covered several square miles of territory without treeing more than a possum or two.

So the panthers were gone but the stories about them were not. After supper the men would sit on the porch and smoke and cough and spit and tell tales. For a person getting ready to make a living by recording stories, this was a wonderful experience, staying on Grandma's Farm. If the people in charge of my life had formed a committee to decide where I would go at this stage of my time, they couldn't have picked a better place than Grandma Hale's and the farms around it. With their hard-working, wet-sweating, dry-talking, yarn-spinning, crooked-grinning folks.

One particular panther story has stayed with me from that time. You understand a panther is a mountain lion, puma, cougar, all the same animal. These big cats once padded over most of my state. They survive in the south and west parts of Texas. They are admired by environmentalists and naturalists and cursed by many ranchers. Cougars will kill lambs, calves, fawns, goats. This is a cat that may measure ten feet from nose to end of tail.

In the stories I listened to, the panther was almost always referred to as being female. Sometimes I heard one called "it" but never "he." This story I first heard at Grandma Hale's but I can't remember who the narrator was. Here it is, the best I can reconstruct it:

"A bunch of us met at Liberty School to set up a search for a lost baby. It was a Culberson. That middle girl of the Culbersons, Millie, she and her husband had a baby ten months old, just a crawler. Millie was at the barn gathering eggs and she turned around and the baby was gone. Just disappeared. They looked, and looked, and couldn't turn up any sign, so they called us in to help. They gave us all a certain part of the country to look in, and we went in pairs. I had Toby Williams with me, that went to war later on and was killed in France. It wasn't freezing weather but it was cold enough if that baby was outside somewhere, she might not make it. We had carbide lights, like for hunting at night. They gave me and Toby the Big Sandy bottom from Liberty School down to the bridge at John Ballard's. We commenced walkin' about an hour past dark and stayed out the whole night. We walked the bottom three times on both sides and never saw a thing. Then, about dawn, just enough light that you could see across the creek, I felt Toby give a jerk on my sleeve. He told me to stop and not move. He said, 'Look a little to your right by that big sycamore if you want to see the biggest panther in Palo Pinto County.' Well, she was a big one, for sure. Sittin' straight up, just like an old tabbycat on the kitchen floor, and lookin' at us. I'd say she was a hundred and twenty-five feet from us. Only gun we had was Toby's twenty-two target he hunted squirrels with. He said, 'You reckon I ought to shoot her?' I said, 'Lord no, that little old bullet would just sting her and make her mad at us.' I told him what we needed to do was start backin' up, real slow, and not run. So we commenced to back up, and ever time we'd make five yards, the panther would follow us about the same distance. But she wouldn't close in, and she didn't sneak up, she'd just walk along easy, and watch us. I whispered to Toby that I didn't think she was goin' to jump us and maybe we'd be all right if we just kept movin'. Toby said, 'I wonder how she'd feel about me turnin' around and movin' frontways.' He said it was a good half mile back down to John Ballard's and John had that new fence and he wasn't sure he could get through four strands of bob wire walkin' backwards. But he didn't turn frontways. He kept goin' backwards. Then I begun to notice somethin' funny. Ever few steps that panther would turn around and look behind her, back toward where we first saw her. I told Toby to stop, because I wanted to check somethin.' When we stopped the panther stopped but when we didn't start up again, the panther turned and walked back in the opposite direction. She'd take a few steps, turn, stop, and look at us. I told Toby I said, 'Toby, I think that panther wants us to follow her. It looks to me like she's tryin' to tell us somethin'.' He said, 'What would a panther have to tell?' I said I didn't know but I wanted to find out. I told Toby to come on and we took several steps toward the panther, instead of away from her, and it was just like I figured. She went on, when we followed her. When we stopped, she'd stop and wait. She still kept her distance. She wouldn't let us gain on her but she wouldn't let us lose her, either. We must have followed that panther a quarter of a mile up the creek. We came to a big elm tree that had shed all its leaves and I happened to see a little spot of red, like paper, or cloth, stickin' out from under the leaves. I kicked at it and knocked some of the leaves aside and it was that Culberson baby, wearin' a red dress, layin' there all covered up. Toby said, 'Well, she's dead.' I got down and took a good look and I told Toby if she was dead she was takin' a long time to stop breathin'. She wasn't anything but sound asleep. We got her up and brushed her off and looked her over and couldn't find one thing the matter with her except she wanted her mama. All of a sudden I remembered the panther and looked for her but she was gone, and we never did see her again. When we were carryin' the baby home we tried to figure out what all had happened. It was plain the panther had led me and Toby to where the baby was sleepin', so we'd find her and she'd be safe. But there was other things I never did get straight in my head. A couple of days later we walked the creek again, to check, and judged it to be about a mile and a half from the Culberson place to where we found the baby. Ain't no baby ten months old gonna crawl that far. Besides, that's pretty raw country. It's bottom, with thickets and thorns and briars. Kid crawl through there, she'd be all scratched up. She wasn't scratched anywhere. Plus, she was on the wrong side of the creek. Is a baby that can't walk gonna swim across creeks? Panthers stealin' babies, that ain't nothin' new. But if this panther stole the baby and carried her a mile and a half up the bottom, how come she didn't show signs of gettin' carried? A panther's not gonna stand up on her hind legs and hold a baby in her arms like a human person. So she carried the baby in her mouth, sure, but we couldn't see a tooth mark anywhere on that baby, not on her hide or in her clothes. Her mama couldn't get a sound out of her, when she'd ask where she'd been and how she spent the night. Course a baby that size ain't gonna make no speeches but you'd think a little adventure like she had would get into her memory pretty deep, but we couldn't see it did. The baby being covered with leaves and grass, that's usual with panthers. They'll rake up leaves and sticks with their claws, and cover a baby up real snug. They're sure mysterious."

That's the sort of stuff I lived on when we were in the country. Tales about panthers, wolves, great snakes. They were told for the truth and I believed them. It pleased me to believe them. Baby-stealing panthers occurred again and again in such stories. These were always the very largest panthers, the biggest ever seen by the storyteller. No half-grown panther was allowed to get into a story. These tales all left questions hanging and there were no answers and this was tantalizing. The unexplained mysteries kept me awake long after the storytellers had turned in. But I didn't mind. I *wanted* to be tantalized. I liked wondering about the mysteries.

Why would a panther steal a baby? Why was it always a baby girl that a panther stole? Did it want to raise the baby as its own? Make a panther-girl of her? How did the panther carry the baby without hurting her? Did the baby ride on the panther's back? Why weren't babies stolen by panthers ever frightened? Why were they never harmed? Why did the panther lead the men to the baby? There were no answers. "Panthers are sure mysterious." They surely were, and they seemed close around me, still out there. When we walked in the pasture I always expected that someone would touch my arm and tell me, "Look a little to your right if you want to see the biggest panther in Palo Pinto County."

I stayed on a permanent high in that wonderful place. Collecting tales. Roaming creeks. Hunting rabbits with real hunting dogs. And when fall came, my mother made an announcement almost too good to believe. She said Ima Ruthie and I would not have to go to school.

While I was in this state of euphoria, I expect my parents and my sister Maifred were in the opposite condition. Because we had been dispossessed.

When a man is defeated, and there is no other place to go, he goes home. That's what my father did, took us to his mother's farm where he knew we wouldn't be turned away. Grandma Hale was gone by then but her youngest daughter, Ruth, was still on the farm and operating it with her husband. He was John Campbell, a tall, straight Arkansas man. They had two children.

Grandma's house always seemed beautiful to me. It was not beautiful. It wasn't a shack but it was the first cousin to one. An unpainted frame structure of four rooms, with a porch and a shed kitchen. A fenced yard of bare dirt that was swept daily the same as the house. Mesquites near the fence. A storm cellar with a great mound of earth on top and a heavy wooden door.

Beds were everywhere in that house. They had to be, after we arrived. Nine people in four rooms. The astonishing thing to me now is, Aunt Ruth and her family were evidently glad to see us move in. I don't understand how they could have been but they seemed to be. Maybe they were lonesome and craved company.

I had thought Glen Rose with its rocky cliffs and dinosaur tracks was in the neighborhood of a paradise but being at Grandma's was even better, since we didn't have to go to school. When all our cousins trudged off with their books and tablets and Ima Ruthie and I stayed home, I decided we were being rewarded for doing something fine. For singing in church, maybe. Or for not missing a single night of Uncle Cleveland's revival. When I found out the real reason, I was disappointed.

The only school within a reasonable distance was a one-room, somewhat decrepit institution called Unity, about three miles from Grandma's. Our mother did not want Ima Ruthie and me to go there. She thought we'd be better off staying home than attending a one-teacher country school sitting on the bank of Barton Creek. The time would come when I would resent that decision. I discovered that people who attended one-teacher country schools eventually developed a pride in it and remained proud of it always, and so I felt deprived. But at the time the decision was made I was all in favor of staying out.

We did go to Unity on Sundays sometimes because church was held there.

When Ima Ruthie was ten, she went an entire year to Sunday School without missing one time. They gave her a pin and called her name from the pulpit so she decided to try for two years. She made the two without a miss and went for three and made that. Then she saw long-range possibilities and set her course for ten years. A decade, without missing Sunday School.

Maintaining Ima Ruthie's record was a problem after we moved to the farm because the country churches in the area didn't hold Sunday School regularly. So we were forever rustling around, looking for Sunday Schools. This was a hardship on a family wallowing in poverty but our mother wasn't about to oppose an effort that had anything to do with church.

We were then still members of the Methodist church at Glen Rose. We didn't join a new church when we went to Grandma's because no Methodist church was near. The Methodists in Texas have never been strong on organizing country churches. So Ima Ruthie attended a lot of Sunday Schools that weren't Methodist. Our mother didn't mind her going to

Sunday School with Baptists or Presbyterians, just as long as she didn't join their church or take up their habits.

In fact, Uncle Cleveland Autry was a Baptist and married to my mother's sister, so we had Baptists in the family without any ill effect. But I still believe my mother would have felt more comfortable if that great revival at Glen Rose had been held by a Methodist.

The upshot of Ima Ruthie's Sunday School habit was that we did a considerable lot of traveling on weekends. Not far, by present measure, but it had to be done weekly. On Saturdays we would often leave Grandma's and go in search of a country church that had promised to hold Sunday School the next day.

Sometimes we would go to Aunt Jenny Hale's house. Aunt Jenny was the widow of Tom Hale, one of my father's older brothers. Uncle Tom was gone by this time. All of us loved Aunt Jenny and liked going to her house. She was full of laughter and jokes. The stovepipe in the kitchen could collapse and spew soot all over the linoleum and Aunt Jenny would discover something funny about it and set us laughing. We would leave her house thinking that one of the most comical of all events was a stovepipe falling down in the kitchen.

For purposes of Sunday School, Aunt Jenny's house had one handy feature. It stood about two hundred steps from the front door of Unity School.

The Sunday School at Unity was operated by the Church of Christ. Among Methodists and Baptists, members of the Church of Christ were called Campbellites. I don't believe that was accurate nomenclature but that's what they were called and there's no changing that fact. They got special notice from members of other Christian denominations because they claimed to be the one true church and if you didn't join it, you would go to hell. I'm told that's not now a fair description of the Church of Christ position, but it was the one I was taught by my mother and I accepted it. Before we went to Sunday School at Unity the first time, our mother took Ima Ruthie and me aside and warned us. She said the Campbellites would try to get us to join their church. She said they'd tell us that we were lost, that being a Methodist wasn't good enough, that no Methodist would ever get to the Pearly Gates and into heaven. She said not to pay attention to that because it wasn't true. I believed her, of course. I believed everything she said. I was not able to visualize any sort of paradise that my mother was not qualified to occupy. I told Ima Ruthie that I didn't want to go to heaven anyhow if Mama wasn't going to be there. She said I better shush up and not talk that way.

Here is a scene dear to me:

We were in the old Chevy, on a country road. It was Sunday morning. My mother was driving. My sister Maifred was with her in the front seat, Ima Ruthie and I in the back. Our father was not with us. We were looking for a church so Ima Ruthie could go to Sunday School. We had gone to one place where a Sunday School had been scheduled but it was cancelled. My mother slowed down and looked at the sun. She said it must be getting close to noon. She stopped the car and told us, "Get out. We're going to have Sunday School right here." We said, "But there's no church here." She said, "Yes, there is. The Lord tells us, 'Where two or more of ye gather together in my name, so shall I be there among ye.' Well, there's four of us and that's plenty. The Lord's here with us so let's begin. Ima Ruth, you lead us in a hymn first." So we stood in the middle of a red country road by the hood of a 1922 Chevy and sang "In The Garden," the hymn about walking and talking with Jesus and how the sound of his voice was so sweet the birds hushed their singing. Then my sister Maifred said a nice prayer and asked God to take care of us and keep us safe and give us our daily bread. I suspect now she wanted to ask him to get her out of the country and back to Fort Worth as soon as it was convenient but she didn't say it, at least not out loud. My mother asked if I wanted to say anything and I said the Chevy's engine smelled hot and we better check the

*radiator. She said never mind about the car and opened her Bible
and read the story about Jesus feeding the multitude that time with
two little old fish and five loaves of bread. This was my next-to-
favorite miracle in the Bible. My favorite was the one where he
turned water into wine at the picnic but our mother being a pro-
hibitionist tended to ignore anything with an alcoholic content,
even a Biblical miracle. She would have loved it if Jesus had done
it the other way around, taken wine and turned it into water. The
Sunday School lesson she taught that day in the road—she spun
it off the loaves and fishes—was that the Lord will provide, that
we would survive those strange times and be all right. She gave a
short closing prayer and then, as an afterthought, threw in this:
"Remember the promise in John 3 : 16. 'God so loved the world he
gave his only begotten son, and whosoever believeth in him shall
have life everlasting.' Amen." I counted that last a parting shot at
the Campbellites, a reminder to her children that being a Methodist and believing in Jesus was plenty good enough for a ticket to
heaven. Then we went back to the farm. And that's why Ima
Ruthie didn't miss Sunday School that day.*

Do you know that my sisters do not now remember that
Sunday School conducted by our mother on the road? I attended thousands of Sunday School sessions after that day but
none is as vivid in my recollection as that one, and they don't
remember it.

The agreement was that my mother would help Aunt Ruth
with the housework and my father would help Uncle John
Campbell in the fields and in this way we would try to make a
contribution and pay for our keep. My mother did better at
this than my father. He drifted away from me, after we had
been so close on the Paluxy. I didn't like the way he looked
anymore. He didn't look handsome and smart. I was accustomed to seeing him in a suit with a vest and a white shirt and

tie and a hat with a crisp brim. On the farm sometimes he wouldn't shave for several days and he didn't seem right.

He was not really strong and farm work was hard on him. That summer we spent several days in a creek bottom, pulling corn. Hot and dusty work. I watched my father when he didn't know I was looking. I grieved for him. I had never seen him sweat so. Drops of it came off his nose and his chin. His face was drawn, his mouth set in a grim line. He was pained, physically and in other ways. Days like that drew him down. It is my belief that he never really recovered from them. He wasn't old then. Still in his forties. But working in a cornfield, to feed his family. Nobody paid a living wage for such work. Taking charity, is how he saw it. I know he did.

We made hominy, boiling the corn in a washpot. We went with Uncle John to the gristmill to have yellow corn ground into meal. The men cut cane and we rode the wagon to the syrup mill and came home with buckets of molasses. The women preserved peaches, beets, tomatoes, beans from the garden. We all picked bushels and bushels of dry cowpeas—black-eyes, purple hulls, creams—and threshed them by a method old as agriculture. We'd stuff them into towsacks (burlap bags) and beat the sacks with sticks and hold the bags high and the loose peas fell onto a wagon sheet and the dry light hulls winnowed out and drifted aside in the wind. Then the dry peas went into storage in wooden barrels.

The jars of preserved vegetables and the jams and the jellies were stored down in the storm cellar. The potatoes we dug were spread out over the bottom of a bin in the barn, and bunches of great yellow onions hung above them and were good all winter long.

I've always wanted to submit to a nutritionist a week's account of what we ate at Grandma Hale's, and see how that authority would judge, say, a week-night supper. Supper was the evening meal. Dinner was at noon. Lunch was something in a paper sack.

Supper was served on a table with an oil-cloth cover. The

knives and forks—I hadn't heard yet of silverware, or flat-ware—were kept in a fruit jar in the middle of the table. When the table was set, each place had a plate turned upside-down and a knife, fork, and spoon lying on top of it in a cluster.

There would be no meat for a week-night meal. If you could call anything a main course it would have to be a vege-table. Black-eyed peas, maybe, which might qualify as a main course since they would have a hunk of salt pork in them. But you didn't eat the salt pork. If you speared a hunk of salt pork and put it on your plate and ate it, you would be looked on as a selfish and gluttonous party. Meat was for flavor, not for consumption. On Sundays a chicken might be killed and we would have it fried, with hot biscuits and cream gravy. We never had chicken on week-nights.

But we had yellow cornbread, great iron skillets of it, and plenty of fresh butter and buttermilk. Then there'd be po-tatoes and a jar of preserved beets on the table, probably. Other week-nights instead of the peas we'd have a huge pot of pinto beans. And always some sort of fruit preserves and syrup to "make out your supper." When you were told to make out your supper, that meant if you hadn't yet had as much to eat as you wanted, finish up on syrup and cornbread.

It's customary for country-reared adults to recall the food prepared by their mothers and aunts as nothing but wonder-ful. Beautiful cakes and pies. Succulent hams and flavorful home-cured bacon.

Sumptuous meals in the country are familiar to me only in connection with special days, like Thanksgiving and Christ-mas. But not daily. What we ate in the country was cornbread and beans.

The first time I tasted a succulent ham was when I grew up and went forth and paid my way into a decent restaurant. On Grandma Hale's Farm there was no smokehouse. There was no fine fat hog raised and killed. There was no home-cured bacon to caress the palate. The bacon we ate was greasy and sometimes rancid and it was served with eggs fried so hard one would bounce twice if you dropped it on the linoleum.

The women whose cooking I supposed was the best in creation did not cook all that well. When I was in tennis shoes and overalls, if you had asked me what my favorite dish was I would have said it was my mother's fried chicken. I was certainly shocked, after I'd been gone from home a few years, to discover that she couldn't fry chicken worth a damn.

But I confess I would never type that last sentence on a page, much less have it printed in a book, if she were yet alive to read it.

Despite staying out of school, my education there in the country went along at a quick pace. I learned to smoke cedar bark with the Barrett boys down the road. I had my first encounter with real tobacco and learned to milk a cow, which I would later regret. I learned how to pick a water moccasin up by its tail and pop its head off. I never actually picked up a moccasin and did that, but Grady Barrett did and I watched him and saw how. I learned how to pick cotton, and forgot it as quick as I could. I began learning how to harness a team of mules but I never finished.

Also at this time I was able to contribute to the education of others. My cousin Garth Campbell was a little younger than I was and I gave him advice and information out of my broad experience. I shared with him my best cuss words from both Glen Rose and Fort Worth, although I doubt he ever had any use for them. I warned him that he should never, in school, let a teacher stand him in front of the room to count by threes. And I passed on to him all the misinformation I had received from Edgar in the boys' restroom at George Clarke School.

Then I fell in love again, this time with a brown-haired girl who attended church at Unity School. She was Aline something. I fell in love, at least, with her back. I was not familiar with her front because if she turned it in my direction I couldn't bear to look at her. So I never knew what her face was like but I didn't care, her back was enough. I wrote her long looping love letters and hid them between two flat rocks down by Grandma's stock tank.

One Sunday night when Ima Ruthie and I had been to Unity, I told Cousin Garth that after church I had taken Aline down on the creek and put it to her on a sandbar. For a lad so young he showed pretty sound judgment. He didn't believe me.

One of the Barrett boys was named Holland. He was my age and we roamed together. Holland's ambition was to be a rodeo cowboy. He began preparing for his career by riding calves. His father's milk cows were out to pasture during the day and their calves were kept in a lot with a split-rail fence.

Holland needed help in catching the calves and holding them while he fixed a bucking strap and climbed aboard. I was the helper. Every now and then he would say, "All right, you take a turn." Meaning he would hold the calf for a change and let me ride. He thought he was doing me a favor. I would get on and try, just to show I was not afraid to do it. Actually I *was* afraid to do it.

I had no hankering to ride anything that bucked and pitched and I was no good at it. Holland could stay on a calf from one end of the lot to the other. Some of these calves were six months old and pretty salty. Generally by the third jump I would be going one way and the calf another and I was forever fetching up against that split-rail fence before I landed. It was a wicked fence. The rails had knots on them, and snags, and coarse splinters, and I didn't enjoy glancing off them. Furthermore I was apt to hit the fence first with my head. Almost every time I hit a thing, my head hit it first. When I would get a lick on the noggin that way I would remember that the doctor in Fort Worth had said I shouldn't get any, ever. The trouble was, I didn't remember it until I had got one.

My mother would often remind me to watch out for blows to the head. When I would leave to go and be with other children she would say, "Now you tell those boys not to hit you on the head." I didn't tell them that. You couldn't tell such things to your peers.

You couldn't admit that you didn't like to ride calves because it hurt, getting thrown against a fence. You couldn't admit you didn't want to fight because getting hit in the head was dangerous for you. Girls could admit things like that but not boys.

Holland Barrett had two or three older brothers and one of them planted two rows of tobacco. For home use, I guess, or maybe just to see if he could get it to grow. These were the only tobacco plants I ever saw sticking out of the ground in Texas.

Holland decided he was going to pull a couple of leaves off that tobacco plant and chew them, and he decided I was going to do it with him. He said it would be a very good thing to do. He said the only reason grown-ups didn't want kids using tobacco was that it was too good to waste on us.

He got the leaves and we went into Conway's pasture, which was a woody section between Grandma's and the Barrett farm. We knew a secret place there. It was a sort of knoll with catclaw bushes around it and a couple of scrub oaks on top and four great boulders in a group. Boulders weighing tons and tons apiece. You could get in among those rocks and hide from anybody in the world except God. This is where we chewed the tobacco.

Green tobacco, fresh off the plant. We wadded some of it up and stuffed it in our mouths and chewed. Almost immediately something curious began happening in mouth. A combination of burns, tingles, and numbness.

Holland asked, "How is it?"

"Good," I lied. "How's yours?"

He nodded and looked off to his left. Tears were in his eyes. Finally he was able to croak a comment. "It's *real* good."

In less than a minute I saw that Holland was having some

kind of strange trouble. He began to separate. He became two boys instead of one. One of him would drift a few inches west, and stay out there quivering. Then he would ease back and pass through his other self and appear on the east side of him. I saw this was an extraordinary trick and I wanted to ask him how he did it but I developed some kind of stomach trouble and began to throw up my dinner.

I wasn't finished with that before the earthquake began. It was major. No minor one could have set those boulders spinning and swapping ends. Everything spun, and flew. The oaks and the catclaws came out of the ground and revolved about my head. Every now and then I would see Holland pass by in a group, three or four of him.

How long these remarkable events lasted I can't say. When we were able to creep we crept to the creek and washed our overalls which were a mess. We spread them on the bank and lay there groaning while they dried.

Too bad I didn't have a similar experience the first time I tried to practice all my other vices. I would have led a life entirely free of bad habits. I could have been a monk.

That night my mother gave me nothing for supper but a bowl of oatmeal and a dose of calomel. She said I looked bilious.

On Grandma's Farm we lived with a great deal of bad information. Some of it was so far from the truth, and presented for consumption in such a creative style, that it approached art. The panther stories, for example. Those were big-league folklore.

Did you know that a dog trotting across a bridge could cause the bridge to start vibrating and the vibration might intensify and cause the bridge to fall? We believed that. I treasured my belief in it. Such a wonderful notion, that an ordinary hound could make a bridge fall without knowing it. A horse or a cow couldn't do it. A team of horses pulling a loaded wagon couldn't do it. A walking dog couldn't do it, nor a running one. An entire pack of large dogs running full out behind a jackrabbit could come thundering across a bridge and they wouldn't produce the smallest quiver.

But any old yard dog that struck a bridge in a trot—look out below.

I've heard mature adults with formal education through the fifth grade at Unity School lecture on this dog-bridge theory. They held that there's something unique about the rhythm of a dog's trot and it would set up a vibration critical to the structure of bridges.

I enjoyed seeing my old friend Red Dog trotting across a bridge I knew. He'd be half asleep, thinking about some nice hole in the ground. He'd get ten feet the other side when this curious noise would cause him to pause and he'd look back and see the bridge falling. And he'd think, "Now whatever caused *that* to happen?"

It didn't occur to me to wonder why we didn't hear of bridges falling every day behind trotting dogs. Still, when we were out with the dogs and came to a bridge we didn't let them trot across. We held them back and made them walk, or shoo'd them across in a lope.

We also believed that highly poisonous creatures were everywhere around us, looking for a chance to bite or sting us to death.

The kind of tarantula common in Texas is practically harmless, but this great hairy-legged spider looks fierce and we counted it even fiercer than it looks. We believed the tarantula stalked across the roads and fields in search of a person to leap on and bite and if one got you, you might as well get on your horse and ride to the undertaker's. We always gave a tarantula a wide berth because the thing was able to jump forty feet. I never saw one leap an inch but I was taught forty feet and I stayed with it. All my life I have been able to tell instantly when a thing is forty feet long or forty feet distant. I got that capability from my early years of staying always forty feet from a tarantula.

The last time I saw a tarantula a country boy of about ten had it in a shoe box along with six or eight others. He would amaze his elders by poking his bare hand in the box and stir-ring the spiders around. Said he hadn't been able to get one to bite him yet.

I can see now that on the farm we were forever being afraid of the wrong things. At the same time, in supreme ignorance, we often charged into the company of creatures that could in-deed harm us.

In the matter of insects, we called it an entertaining sport to fight wasps and yellowjackets and hornets and bumblebees. We would whittle paddles and knock down wasp nests and see how many wasps we could whip dead with our paddles be-fore one of them stung us.

It was thought a mark of courage to take several stings and hurt over them and laugh about the swelling. We would be surprised to learn, as adults, that wasp stings can kill. We would not have believed it if we had read that in the 1930s.

We were even afraid of the wrong spiders. I remember sit-ting in the privy at Grandma's, just at dusk, afraid to go out, because the evening before we had seen a tarantula creep across the yard near the outhouse. If I went out, in near darkness, there'd be no way I could see well enough to keep forty feet from a tarantula.

So I stayed a long time in the privy, until somebody came with a lantern to get me out. I felt safe from tarantulas in that little house. The likelihood is that while I sat there feeling safe, at least one black widow spider hung just beneath the wooden seat, within inches of my bare behind. Black widow bites can make people seriously sick and these spiders are often found nesting in outhouses. Probably I'd have been safer from spiders with my bare hand stuck in a shoe box of tarantulas.

What we feared most in the woods, not counting panthers, was rattlesnakes. At least this was a justified fear.

But we felt more than fear about rattlers. We felt respect, admiration, and a consuming curiosity. This was true of adults as well as children. At night on the porch the men told of seeing huge rattlers, back in times when snakes were big-

113 / THE FARM

ger and bolder. Snakes eight feet long "with thirty-two rat-
tles and a button." They told of rattlers swallowing full-grown
jackrabbits. They told of lying in the brush and watching the
mating rituals of these giant reptiles, how they danced on
their tails and entertwined their bodies, "big around as a man's
thigh." Any visitor to the farm who brought a big-snake
story to tell was guaranteed an attentive audience.

A man I remember as Mr. Ransom came one time and told
about the night he slept with a rattlesnake. He had been trap-
ping on the Brazos River that winter and was caught in a bliz-
zard. He built a fire on a knoll and wrapped up in his blankets
and was warm. About midnight he came awake gradually and
was aware of a considerable weight on his chest and stomach.
What had happened, while he slept a six-foot rattlesnake had
crawled slowly into his bedroll and coiled up on his middle,
looking for warmth.

There was no point in wondering how he knew it was a
rattler. It had to be a rattler or else there would have been
no story, no worthwhile event. Don't ask, either, what a six-
foot rattlesnake was doing out on a night like that in the
middle of winter, when it ought to have been in hibernation
in a deep hole.

You understand why Mr. Ransom was perplexed. He had
to lie still and consider. He wanted to throw off his blankets
and spring up and get away, but any sudden move was certain
to result in a snake bite. So he moved very, very slowly. He
moved only his arm and hand, working the hand up toward
the snake. It didn't stir. A snake is sluggish in winter, remember. It remained still when he touched its body with the tip
of his fingers. He'd heard a snake liked to be stroked, lightly.
He stroked its coils. In the stroking he was able to picture
how the snake was lying. Where its tail was. Where its deadly
head was.

What a wonderful scene that was to me. I was there, with
Mr. Ransom, by the fire on the knoll. I could see his hand
beneath the blankets, moving slowly, rubbing that snake
coiled on his stomach. What a man.

When his fingers felt the snake's neck, felt the place where the slender neck began to flare into the awful triangular head, Mr. Ransom grabbed.

He made us feel what he felt. Made us see it. We could see the desperate writhing of the rattler beneath the blanket. We could feel the coils beating and sliding on our stomachs, just the way Mr. Ransom felt them. We could hear the piercing buzz of the snake's rattlers, and feel their electric touch on our bellies. We could see Mr. Ransom come rising out of his bedroll, holding the rattler high, pulling his skinning knife and lopping off the triangular head. Mr. Ransom, who slept with a rattlesnake.

The man who escaped an encounter with a rattler that way was a hero but a greater one was the man who did not escape, who got bitten. We celebrated his life ever afterward. A person distinguished in no other way could achieve distinction by surviving a rattlesnake bite. Even a small rattler would do, but the bigger it was the more celebrated the victim.

Ima Ruthie and I once viewed a young man who had been bitten. I chose that verb with care. We viewed him. We didn't meet him or visit him or just happen to see him.

This was in the town of Thurber, about five miles west of Grandma's Farm. Ima Ruthie and I went there for the same reason we went anywhere, to find her a Sunday School. We stayed with Aunt Minnie Hale, the widow of another of our father's brothers, George. Aunt Minnie was a slender little person who kept her hair pulled tight against her head and over her ears and fixed in a knot at the back of her neck. She always looked just exactly that way, like a pioneer woman. She died only recently, not long before her one-hundredth birthday.

Sometimes we would stay with her for an entire week and kill two Sundays in one visit. Between Sunday Schools, Ima Ruthie and I would roam the town and listen to all the local news. The best news we heard was that a boy had been bitten by a large rattler and he lived right there in Thurber and it was possible to view him. And the snake, as well. It had been killed.

Thurber was a small town and all we needed to do to find the right house was follow the crowd. The house had a picket fence. The dead snake was draped over a post just to the right of the front gate. I remember the rattler as being six feet long. That doesn't mean it was really that long, necessarily. Rattlesnakes do grow to that size but many four- and five-foot rattlers were called six-footers in stories told about them. Sort of the same as fish, which get so much bigger two or three weeks after they're caught.

A dozen or more people were standing in a semicircle near the snake, studying and commenting. Others were moving slowly in and out of the house. The front door was open. People entered in a loose file and presently emerged by a side door. They were going in to view the boy. It reminded me of the way people had moved in and out of Uncle Brinky's lumberyard in Stephenville to view corpses before funerals.

Ima Ruthie said we ought not to miss this chance so we worked our way into the parade. People in the line spoke in hushed tones. When they got near where the boy was, they didn't speak at all. He was about fourteen, I think. He was in a high bed beneath a white sheet. It was said he had been bitten on the leg, which was covered up.

He did not appear to be in pain. As we passed and stared, he gave each of us a benign smile. No word was spoken when we were in his room. But in the yard it was told that he had been helping his father build fence and after the snake struck him his father had killed it with a mesquite post. His father then cut an X on the bite and sucked the wound and spit out the blood.

We returned to Aunt Minnie's and told her what we had seen and heard and she was very interested. It was talked about all during supper, and frequently for a month, and occasionally for years and years, how we viewed the boy who was bitten by the rattlesnake, and how he smiled at us.

We believed mountain boomers were as poisonous as rattle-snakes. Mountain boomer is the name we called the collared lizard. This is a large lizard—more than a foot if you count its tail—that's common in West Texas. It lives under rocks and has a snakelike head and a bad disposition.

If you disturb one it may chase after you, and up on its hind legs, at that. Being chased by a mountain boomer, in combination with the belief that it would kill you if it caught you, that was sure stimulating.

We believed that if a centipede crawled around your leg, your leg would rot and fall off. If a snapping turtle grabbed your hand, he wouldn't let go until it thundered. If a horned toad spit in your eye, that eye would go blind.

Our mother would never feed her family fish and milk at the same time because she believed they would poison us. Being a doctor's daughter, she was thought to be a good, practical physician. On one occasion, memorable to us all, she certainly enhanced that reputation.

That was when Tommie Ann Campbell got sick and had a convulsion on Grandma Hale's Farm. Tommie was the daughter of Aunt Ruth and Uncle John Campbell. She was three. I don't know what disease she had but she went into a spasm. She became rigid and gray.

All of us thought she was dying. I certainly did. My mother shouted for a washtub. She ordered cold water to be put in it. Then she called for the kettle which was kept full and heating on the stove all day. "Put in hot water," she ordered, and hot water was poured in. She held the baby across her knees. She reached into the tub to test the water. "More hot, more hot," she ordered. When the water was the temperature she wanted, she put Tommie in the tub. Or she tried. That baby would not bend, to fit in. She was absolutely stiff, and turning black. I thought, Well, Tommie's gone. Because I had never seen a live person who looked that bad. In fact, I had seen dead ones in Uncle Brinky's lumberyard that looked better than Tommie did. My mother bathed her in the tepid water, using a towel to bring up water, squeezing it out on the baby. Gradually Tommie began to relax, and could be put down in the tub. Her color improved. She cried.

Today Tommie is an attractive grandmother, tall and straight and graceful. My mother has always gotten credit for saving her life. Maybe she did, by knowing to immerse the sick child in tepid water, not hot or cold.

Saving the life of a baby she loved must have been rewarding. Especially so in the light of our position there on the farm as nonpaying guests. It was not ever mentioned, of course, but I know my mother felt that after Tommie's illness, she had paid our room and board. She was a woman who kept accounts.

The Sheep Ranch

IMA RUTHIE *and I were walking into Granbury from the sheep ranch. The distance was between three and four miles. I was feeling pretty good. I had been getting stronger lately. I could use Uncle Grover Oxford's double-bit ax to chop through eight-inch mesquite logs and cut the pieces into short sticks and split them on the chopping block and carry them to the woodbox by the kitchen stove. I had gotten able to stand before a mirror. I wouldn't look at the face of the strange boy but I looked at his upper arms. I could fold my arms across my chest and squeeze and my biceps would spread against the backs of my fingers and show definite signs of bulging. When we went into Granbury I would practice my new way of walking, a little the same as an ape. I would carry my arms slightly bent and swinging almost in front of me. I would tuck my chin so that my neck was a bit bowed. My shoulders would take turns dipping with every step, which enabled me to go along in a wonderful swagger. I had seen bigger boys in Granbury walking that way and it was just the right way. I had also learned to squirt spit between my front teeth, but not yet for much distance. When Ima Ruthie and I were walking into town, these two mean fellows came out of a pasture and stopped us. They were old, sixteen or seventeen, and much bigger than I was. They used cuss words on us and they grabbed*

Ima Ruthie and pulled at her clothes. They said they would do bad things to her. I said, "Take your hands off my sister." They laughed at me. One said, "Get rid of him. Hit him. Hit him in the head." The shortest one took a swing at me but I ducked under it and buried my right fist in his middle. "Oof!" he said, and doubled over and put his hands to his stomach and sank to the ground, gasping. The bigger one said, "Why, you little . . ." He lunged at me but missed because I dodged, alertly, and gave him a left to the jaw and then a lightning right to the chin and he went down and was still in the dirt. The first one by this time was breathing better and I pulled the bigger one to a sitting position and slapped him awake and I said, "Now listen to this. My sister and I will be walking along this road every Sunday morning for a good while. If you ever see us coming, you turn around and go the other way. Do you understand that?" They said they did, and they got up and slunk off into the mesquite and never gave us any trouble again. They knew better.

We did walk those three or four miles into Granbury from the sheep ranch. We went every Sunday so I don't have to tell you why we went.

Granbury is thirty-three miles southwest of Fort Worth. It is the county seat of Hood County but it was just another little country town when we moved to the ranch. We left Grandma Hale's Farm and went to Granbury to help my mother's brother, Uncle Grover Oxford. He was in a lot of pitiful trouble.

It strikes me now you may be hoping that pretty soon the fortunes of my family in these chronicles would sink to their lowest point, so we could start back up. Well, we have arrived. The sheep ranch was the bottom. At least it was for me, because I thought our father had deserted us.

He didn't go to the ranch with us. I don't know where he went. I know he didn't stay on the farm. My sister Maifred didn't go to the ranch, either. She stayed with friends in another place. I had the uneasy feeling that our family was breaking up.

The ranch was where Uncle Grover Oxford lived. It was not his ranch. But he was a cowboy kind of person and he took care of the livestock on that place in return for rent on the house.

I liked Uncle Grover the most, of all my mother's brothers. I admired the way he walked, as if he always wore boots and chaps even when he had on holey shoes and ragged khakis. I liked how he talked, so slow. And moved, so quick, like a rodeo roper tying a calf. He was married to Aunt Maude, a sweet-faced lady who had three children. She also had cancer and was dying in a hospital in Fort Worth. Uncle Grover worked in Granbury. He asked our mother to come stay on the ranch and take care of his children. All three were below school age and one was a baby boy.

When I found out what kind of work Uncle Grover did in town I was disappointed. He was a dishwasher in a cafe. I'm glad I didn't have to see him doing that. I preferred seeing him on a horse. He looked natural and good on a horse.

He would get up early every morning, around four o'clock, and go off to town and when he finished work he would go to Fort Worth to be with his wife. When he got home his children would be asleep already and days and days would pass this way and he wouldn't get to see them.

I had very little fun on that ranch. In fact, for the first time in my life, I got unhappy and worried. Through all our previous troubles, I had somehow stayed removed from them, I think mainly because the places where we endured them were, for me, good places. The sheep ranch was not.

The house was a small square frame structure on a bare yard with a fence to keep the sheep out. I couldn't see why we needed to keep out the sheep because nothing was in that yard they could have eaten or damaged. Not a sprig of grass. Not one flower or shrub or small tree. Not even a weed.

The nearest tree must have been half a mile from the front

gate. The house stood on top of a broad and empty rise. I suppose it was located there to catch a breeze in summer but in winter the crest of that rise was cold without mercy. The wind never rested. It had scoured the yard. Not a pebble was left, or enough dust to make a swirl, because the wind had blasted it all away. We were accustomed to windy places but the wind here was hostile, it was the enemy. It punished us. It pushed and shoved and whistled and moaned. It rattled the windows and popped the clothes on the line and banged the gates. It withered the spirit inside us.

There was no handy place to hide from that wind. The ranch didn't even have a barn, just a sheep shed with one end closed in for a feed and tack room. Sometimes Ima Ruthie and I would take our little cousins down the slope to a low part of the pasture that had a mesquite thicket. We would get back in that thicket, deep as we could go, and just sit there where the wind couldn't find us.

We were living a great sadness, waiting for Aunt Maude to die. My mother tried to keep us encouraged but she was not able to hide her distress. She prayed far too much to suit me. I knew that was a sign of great trouble.

She was forever washing in that place. She scrubbed clothes on a washboard and boiled them in lye soap. When she thought she was alone she would close her eyes, her wet sudsy hands resting on a washboard, and pray in desperation. I hated it when she did that. It meant things were really bad, or else that much praying wouldn't be necessary.

One day I realized that I hadn't heard Ima Ruthie sing in a long time. I asked her to sing. I said I would sing with her. We could sing "Living For Jesus" and she could do that pretty harmony on the chorus. But she didn't want to. She said the strings on her uke were broken. Which they were, but that wasn't why she didn't want to sing. It just wasn't a time for singing.

Some afternoons, between meals at the cafe, Uncle Grover would get to come home and see his children. Then he would go down into the mesquite and chop wood and haul it to the house. That mesquite was our only source of fuel.

I wanted to go with him, talk to him. I was missing my father fiercely and Uncle Grover was the only man that had spoken to me in weeks, and he hadn't spoken much. He didn't want to talk. He was tormented by his troubles.

From a distance I would watch him attack the mesquite with his ax. He was a good axman and he worked with a fury. It was as if those trees represented his frustrations and he was trying to chop them away. Once after he had been swinging the ax with special violence I saw him drop to the ground, put his head down, and sob.

I understood that, even though I couldn't have gotten it into words. His load was almost too heavy. His young wife was dying. Those three babies in that cold house were about to become motherless. His pay was not enough for groceries, much less heavy medical bills. And Christmas was coming, and those children believed in Santa Claus. How could any man stand up under all that without crying?

Prospects for Christmas sure weren't looking too good, for any of us. I had started trying to accept that we would spend it without my father. My mother had quit talking about when he was coming, and I had quit asking about it. Ima Ruthie and I didn't even talk about it. I was afraid to ask her. I was afraid she'd say, Yes, he's gone.

Then suddenly, two days before Christmas, my mother said he was coming.

I could hear the familiar knocking of the engine before the old Chevy came into sight on the road. So maybe it was true. Maybe he was coming. I ran to open the gate. I could see the plume of steam from the leaky radiator. He was turning in, and I saw the front door and how it was wired up, the way he patched it when the latch quit working. At last I could see his long neck and his face, grinning at me through the crack in the windshield.

Then his skinny arm came out of the open window and

made a wide crook, so I could run into it. He held me there for a time, my father who had left us, but who hadn't left us after all and had come back. I discovered there by the sheep ranch gate that a person can cry out of gladness, and not be able to stop.

You ought to have seen the back seat of that old car. The things he brought, we could not believe they were possible.

He brought my mother a new dress and a nice heavy sweater. He brought toys for our little cousins. A coat for Ima Ruthie, and a set of new ukulele strings. For Uncle Grover he brought a nice cowboy shirt, and it fit, and made him smile. I wonder how long it had been since that poor man smiled. For me, an air rifle. An *air rifle!* With two bags of BB's, whispering to me in their delicious rattle. I wonder if you can imagine how near to impossible it was for me to get a new air rifle that Christmas. And yet, there it was. I took it to bed with me and slept with it.

He brought even more. A turkey, and a ham, and a roast. Fresh cranberries and a pumpkin. Bags of sugar and flour. Stalks of celery. Apples and oranges and bananas and marshmallows and popcorn and candy wrapped in tinfoil.

He brought presents for my sister Maifred and the next morning we went with him to wherever she was and brought her to the ranch and we were all together again.

We took Uncle Grover's ax and went across the road and cut a little cedar tree and fixed a stand out of boards and put it in the corner of that pitiful house. The girls took tinfoil from the candy and cut it into strips and made icicles for the tree. They popped popcorn and strung it by needle and thread and draped it on the branches. They cut strips out of the colored sections of the mail-order catalog and made paper chains with flour and water paste and decorated the tops of the doors and windows.

They made a crooked star out of pasteboard, and covered it in tinfoil, and fixed it on the highest place on the tree. This was a lopsided tree. But on that Christmas Eve it was beautiful in the gleam of a kerosene lamp.

It was beautiful also because we stood around it and sang songs with Ima Ruthie leading us, strumming her ukulele with the new strings. This was the best Christmas I ever had.

That night, lying in bed with my air rifle, a sound came to me that I had not heard in a long time. It was a good sound, but familiar only in a distant way.

It was my mother, laughing.

Before my father came back, when Ima Ruthie and I walked into Granbury to Sunday School, she carried her Nice Shoes under her arm in a paper sack. She walked in the same thing I did—ragged tennis shoes. When we got near the church she would change, and put her old shoes in the sack and hide it in the weeds. Then on the way home she would retrieve the sack and change back to her old shoes. I thought of her as having Nice Shoes, capitalized that way.

We were all proud of those shoes. She got them when we were on Grandma's Farm. My father acquired them somehow. He went off and stayed a day or two and came back with those shoes. They were in a box that looked as if he had wrapped it himself.

All of us gathered around while Ima Ruthie unwrapped the box and showed the shoes nestled in tissue paper. Like jewels. We felt as if each of us had gotten new shoes. They were cream-colored, and fit just exactly. My father had sold a lot of shoes in stores and knew how to buy them even when the person they were for wasn't present.

Nobody questioned that Ima Ruthie was the one to get the Nice Shoes. They weren't really for her. They were for Sunday School, to prevent the record from falling. Her record had become a sort of symbol of family respectability and my father had gotten ashamed to see her go off to church in ragged tennis shoes.

That term, tennis shoes, seems a misnomer now. In the time I am talking about, any rubber-soled shoe with a canvas top was called a tennis shoe. We didn't associate such footwear with the game of tennis. It was simply what we could afford.

I remember tennis shoes being advertised for $1.29 a pair, and high-tops, at that. We wore them in snow and ice the same as we did in summer. I was surprised when I found out that tennis was a game played by privileged people. To me it had always meant cheap shoes.

I wondered how on this earth my father got those shoes, which must have cost almost five dollars. True, he'd always had a way of coming home with surprising gifts, but these shoes he acquired at a time when we were flat penniless.

And then came that incredible Christmas on the sheep ranch. All that stuff he brought must have been worth $100 or more. I couldn't help thinking he might have stolen it.

After Aunt Maude died, Uncle Grover got a job on another ranch and took his children there and we moved back to Fort Worth for a while. Ima Ruthie and I went to school for half a year.

This was the year the Lindbergh baby was kidnapped and killed. Lindbergh was the greatest of all American heroes, even greater to me than Cox, the right fielder on the Cats. His flight across the ocean was the first news story I was ever interested in. The kidnapping may have been the second. This was the first time I had heard and seen newsboys—men, actually—hurrying through the streets, selling extra papers, shouting headlines. It was fearsome but exciting. The men even came along the street where we lived.

"EX-truh! EX-truh PAY-puh! LIN-bergh BAY-bee KID-napped! EX-truh PAY-puh!"

When school was out we went back to Grandma Hale's Farm for a few weeks. My sister Maifred was staying with kinfolks in the little town of Eastland, ninety miles west of Fort Worth. One day I had gone down to Grandma's mailbox on the road to wait for Mr. Boles. He was the rural mail carrier. The adults spoke of Claude Boles as if he were wealthy. By our standards I suppose he was. All during the Great Depres-

sion he had that government job, which may have paid
$100 a month. I'd hear my folks saying, "You take a fellow
like Claude Boles. He doesn't even know we're having a
Depression."

On this day Mr. Boles brought a letter to my mother. It
was from my sister Maifred, writing to tell us that she had
found a job, working for the Eastland County *Weekly Record*.
So all of us moved to Eastland because my sister had a job
there that paid five dollars a week.

Home Town

I HAVE ALWAYS BEEN PICKY about names and I didn't like the name of the town, Eastland. It didn't fit. The town is in the west part of the state so a better name would have been Westland. But the worst thing was that Eastland sat exactly between two awful towns with really wonderful names. Ranger was ten miles east and Cisco was the same distance west. You would have to think a long time before you came up with two better names for West Texas towns than Ranger and Cisco.

I used past-tense verbs in the preceding paragraph because Ranger and Cisco are not now the terrible places they were when I was growing up in Eastland. Those towns improved as I got older. I discovered the same thing happened to Eastland, where we lived until I got through high school. Its population then was about 4,500.

Those of us going through Eastland's school thought that our most serious disadvantage was living so near such dreadful places as Cisco and Ranger. Their principal fault was that they were always whipping us in football. No town could have done anything to convince us any quicker that it was a bad place.

The summer I came out of high school, Ranger began to improve. I stayed there a few days and was astonished that everybody I met was perfectly decent. Cisco was slower but it improved, as well, as soon as I got acquainted with it. By the time I'd been out of school two years, I considered that both Ranger and Cisco had undergone a total transformation and were favorable places. At first I supposed the improvement was the result of Eastland's influence, situated as it was an equal distance from the two towns and giving off good examples daily. But the friends I eventually made in both Ranger and Cisco confessed to me that, when we were all growing up, they looked on Eastland as a strange and snobbish town, populated by peculiar folks who somehow improved with age.

Eastland is the county seat of the county with the same name, which has nothing to do with a point of the compass. It came from Captain William Mosby Eastland who fought in the Texas Revolution and later became a Texas Ranger. If the history teachers I had in Eastland ever mentioned Captain Eastland, I wasn't listening. We didn't identify in any way with that gent. I doubt he ever rode a horse across the county. When he was alive he lived near La Grange, far, far away between Houston and San Antonio where nobody who lived in Eastland had ever been.

So our town wasn't famous on account of Captain Eastland. It was famous instead on account of a lizard.

Didn't we have a talent for finding famous places to live? Look at Glen Rose, with its dinosaurs and miraculous waters. Fort Worth, with the world's greatest baseball team. And then Eastland, with its lizard.

We called it a horned toad. Or horned frog. Or *horny* frog, most of the time. Actually it's the Texas horned lizard, *Phrynosoma cornutum*. A curious little creature. The biggest ones grow to seven inches if you count the tail. They are common over a great part of Texas and they're practically everywhere in the western part.

When Eastland County put up a new courthouse in 1897, the county commissioners caused a horned frog to be sealed into the cornerstone, along with the documents deposited there to reflect the time the courthouse was built. Horned frogs are tough. They eat ants. They look reptilian and act fierce. They squirt blood out of their eyes and in that way scare enemies bigger than they are, including human girls. They endure all manner of natural hardships such as drouths and sandstorms and boys chunking rocks.

Evidently the county's commissioners felt this creature was a good symbol of the region's frontier spirit. It was said the horned frog could live for years without food or water, even without air. So one of these lizards named Old Rip was cemented into that cornerstone and stayed there thirty-one years. You see how Rip got his name. Rest In Peace.

In 1928 when that cornerstone was opened, Old Rip was still alive.

I didn't believe that when we moved to Eastland but a few years later I got proof that it was true. I got it from Jim Golden. Jim lived in the Connellee Hotel and worked at the power plant on the Leon River. He was a good man, friendly and helpful. I asked around town and was told that Jim was a truthful person in all ways and any time Jim Golden said a thing was true I could go and put it in the bank.

So one day in the Corner Drugstore I asked him: Was it true about Old Rip? Jim said it was. How did he know? He knew, Jim said, because when they opened the cornerstone that time in '28 he was standing right there, and looked into the cavity along with the first ones. And there was Old Rip, blinking his snaky eyes. Looking thirsty, sure, and sleepy, and he'd lost some weight, but he was alive.

Well, there you are. Jim Golden said it.

That little town has produced some things worth talking about. It produced Verna Johnson, the world's best school-teacher. Also Tex Satterwhite, who played with Tommy Dorsey and was one of the best trombone men in the hemisphere. Then the two greatest athletes of all time grew up in Eastland. They were John Garrison and Darrell Tully, but do you think they got any recognition? No. That lizard got it all.

Since I left Eastland I have traveled to Naples, Italy, and London, England, and places even farther flung and when I said I was from Texas people would ask, "Where in Texas?" I would admit Eastland and they would brighten and say, "Isn't that the town where they put the frog in the cornerstone and it lived for thirty years?"

At last I went ahead and got proud of it, since nothing else was to be done. At least we had the most famous *Phrynosoma cornutum* in the universe. I believe if we had got Jim Golden elected president, people would have said he's a fine good man and the best thing our town ever turned out, next to that lizard.

A salary of twenty dollars a month for a girl was enough to impress anybody in West Texas in the early 1930s. A salary. We hadn't had a salary in the family since my father quit the store in Stamford.

He made another deal for a place we could live. Near the high school a family by the name of Hearne was moving out of an orange house, and leaving town. They had a sturdy son, called J.C., who didn't want to leave Eastland because he had a year's eligibility left in football. He wanted to stay there and play his senior year.

His folks owned the house and couldn't sell it so our deal was this: J.C. would live in a back room, and my mother would feed him in return for the rent on the rest of the house. It worked pretty well because J.C. never came into the kitchen the way Mrs. Nichols did in Glen Rose. My mother took his meals to him on steaming plates. J.C. wasn't a great football player but he was easy to get along with and didn't make trouble.

They sent Ima Ruthie and me off to school. Ima Ruthie didn't like it and came home and stayed. She was supposed to be in the seventh grade and I was in the fifth. I didn't like my first day, either. While I was bending down to get a drink out of the fountain, a big kid leaned down and said in my ear, "What's that knot on the side of your head?"

I told him I got hit there with a rock and he said, "Your eye is crooked, too."

I told him I knew about it and he asked me if I was some

kind of smart-mouth. I walked away and didn't look at him. I wondered why it was that boys were always coming up to me and telling me about my physical curiosities, just as if they were telling me something I didn't know. I found boys to be cruel that way. Not girls, though. Girls were always kind to me and I think that's why I was forever falling in love with them. Another thing about girls was, they generally smelled nice and looked as if they'd feel really good, although at this time I had never felt one.

Why Ima Ruthie had this problem with school I don't know. But one day in Eastland she got over it and went to school and she has never stopped. Even when she finished the eleventh grade and they graduated her, she didn't quit. She stayed around and took post-graduate courses. I didn't know a person could take post-graduate work in a public high school but Ima Ruthie did it. She may have invented the idea.

She would later leave that school long enough to get married and have a couple of daughters and even work at jobs that had nothing to do with school. But she went back, and eventually became the secretary to the superintendent of Eastland's school system. As I am writing this sentence, she is sixty-seven years old and officially retired from that position. But she hasn't quit. She still goes to work, just the same as she kept going to school when she graduated. She has seen three generations of kids pass through that school, and has sung every one of her ten thousand songs from the stage of the auditorium, and played her piano at countless functions, and I do not believe she intends ever to quit that place. I think of it as Ima Ruthie's School. I think she does, too.

We lived in that orange house of the Hearnes for about two years. An important thing I did there was to catch diphtheria. A strange man came to our house when I got sick. He pulled my shorts down and I felt a very bad pain in my rear. I was feverish and imagined that Dr. Oxford had finally got me in the kitchen and was cutting off my leg.

The man in fact was Dr. Brown, who would be our family

physician for years to come. He was one of the kindest men I ever knew. The pain I had felt was his needle, pumping serum into me. That was the first time I'd ever been stuck with a needle.

Dr. Brown nailed a sign on our front porch: QUARANTINE, in big red letters. It meant nobody could come into our house. Nobody ever did anyhow but I liked the sign. It was impressive. Children walking to school would see the sign and cross over to the other side of the street and stand a minute and stare at the house.

The school I attended our first year in Eastland was called West Ward. It was a two-story dark red brick building that looked more like a county jail than anything else. The whole time I went there I stayed in love with a brown-haired girl named Billie. One day in the hall she dropped her pencil. I picked it up and handed it to her and she said, "Thanks." That was the only word she ever spoke to me.

Living in Eastland to me was entirely satisfactory. Hard Times, as far as I was concerned, never again got as hard as they were on that sheep ranch. In Eastland we were living in a decent house, and our sister had that five dollars every week from her job. At least she did when the owner of the paper could meet the payroll. Sometimes he couldn't, even though he had just one person to pay. There was no question about what that cash would be spent for. It would help support the family. I doubt my sister ever thought of spending it on herself, and she didn't. From the day she went to work for that little weekly, I thought of her as a breadwinner the same as my father was, and some months she won bread when my father won none.

This doesn't mean that my father stopped working. He worked always. At Eastland he began selling magazines to country people. He would bounce around on country roads and sell subscriptions to a magazine called *Holland's,* and another called *Farm and Ranch.* Country people had no cash to spend on magazines but they had produce. Sweet potatoes,

peanuts, grain, chickens, eggs. My father would swap subscriptions for things like that, then haul them into town and
sell them, take his little cut out of the total and send what was
left to the magazine.

Which was a mighty slow way to get rich but the work did
have the advantage that it involved food. We had plenty to eat
that winter. We didn't have what we wanted but we didn't
go hungry. That was a good year for sweet potatoes and we
had yams until we would see them marching in rows in our
dreams. We wanted to tell him, "Please, don't trade for any
more yams." But we didn't say it, of course. We were happy
that he had something to do, so he could get up in the morning and go forth, and work, and be useful.

I bet I could write you, even now, a dozen different ways to
cook sweet potatoes. Don't worry, I won't do it but I could.
We might have yams every day for two straight weeks and
they wouldn't be fixed the same way twice. I found out that
sweet potatoes sliced thin and fried in an iron skillet were very
good indeed. Since that winter when I was in fifth grade, I
have not sat down at a table where fried sweet potatoes were
served. But in the Hearne house we had them often, and
bragged on our mother for fixing them so well. We had baked
yams, boiled yams, candied yams, yams in a pie. There is a
way to mash sweet potatoes and shape them into patties and
fry them, sort of like hash brown Irish spuds, and they taste
wonderful. When we were flush and could afford a frivolity
like marshmallows, they would be arranged with care on the
top of a sweet potato pudding and served as a dessert, half
melted and browned.

Eastland County is a big peanut-growing place. My father
was forever trading for a bushel or two of peanuts. I would go
to school with my pockets bulging with the things. After
supper at home we would parch peanuts on a flat pan and eat
them for hours. Pecans, as well. We always had fresh pecans.

That was our entertainment, eating. As soon as the table
was cleared at night and the dishes washed, the girls would
start making things to eat again. They would pop popcorn,

and make popcorn balls stuck together with the syrup my father had brought in from the country. They would make divinity candy, and taffy, and something they called buttermilk candy with pecans in it. It was a kind of poor-folks' fudge that didn't require chocolate, which was expensive.

We had never eaten so much. I doubt the diet had much balance but it was strong on volume. I don't know why we didn't every one get fat as butter but we didn't.

I supposed my father was happy again, bringing in all that food for us. Sometimes he *seemed* happy, but I discovered that he was just pretending. The truth was he was ashamed of what he was doing, peddling magazines for sweet potatoes. Actually, chickens were his main source of cash. They could always be sold so he built a two-tier chicken coop and mounted it on the back of that old Chevy. When he had a good day in the country he'd come home with that coop loaded with chickens, squawking and clucking and shedding feathers in the wind.

I thought that looked grand, but he was mortified by it. I learned how he felt when I went with him a few times to sell the chickens at the produce house. He would drive way around the edge of town, to keep people from seeing him. From the time he put the coop on the car, he never drove it downtown again.

Some Saturdays he would take Ima Ruthie or me with him to the country. I loved to go. I was proud of him again. To go out and sell magazines and haul chickens and peanuts, he dressed the same way he dressed when he worked in the store. He wore his suit with a vest and a white starched shirt and necktie, tied just right. And his shoes shined. He might come home with mud or manure on his shoes, but when he left home they were shining and clean.

When I went with him he would let me help catch the chickens he traded for. He almost never stopped at a farmhouse without making some kind of trade. It might be for one fryer, or half a bushel of wheat, or two bales of peanut hay. I loved watching him work. I do think he was happy when he worked.

He had this way of going up to a country house and becoming one of the family without any introduction. Say two women would be sitting on the front porch, shelling peas. He'd come rising out of that old car and first thing he'd say was, "Need any help?"

They'd grin about that. They couldn't help it. He'd go up on the porch and sit down and start shelling peas, and telling mild little jokes, and he'd have them laughing pretty soon. Laughing with their mouths shut. A lot of country women then didn't like to smile or laugh because they had bad teeth, or missing ones in front. When I think of them now I see women laughing, shoulders shaking, with their mouths clamped shut. Not many men came into the lives of women like that, to make them feel like smiling. He was good with women.

Well, with the men, too, and even the dogs. Dogs loved him. I've seen him walk into yards that I wouldn't go in wearing a suit of armor, on account of the mean-looking dogs. He just didn't have any fear of them, and they liked him for it.

One day, late in the afternoon, we walked up to the fence of a cow lot where this old farmer was about to milk. My father said his usual, "Need any help?" and I don't think the farmer thought much of it. He said, "Yeah, you can come in here and milk this cow." He knew my father wouldn't do it, all dressed up like a city dude, and there'd been rain, and the lot was a mess.

My father said, "Be glad to." He shucked his suit coat and handed it to me and rolled up his sleeves and went right on in the lot. I watched his shiny dress shoes sink into the mud and the cow dung. He took off his hat and sailed it right into my hands, with a smooth underhanded flip. He got the bucket from the farmer and squatted down, Indian style, and milked that cow. He buried his head in her flank and it wasn't long before he had foam rising up in the bucket and the old farmer stood there grinning and shaking his head.

When we left the lot and walked to the house, my father carried the bucket of milk with the cats following along to lick up the foam dripping down the bucket's sides. Half an hour later we drove away from there with a dozen chickens in the coop and a sack of shelled corn and two buckets of molasses and I don't know what else, maybe even forty-five or fifty cents in cash.

I believe when he lost himself in people that way, he was happy for a little while. But he would have these bad days, when trouble descended on him and weighed too much.

Ima Ruthie told me this, but not until years after it happened:

She was riding with him in the country and the old Chevy stalled on the road. It was a worn-out car. It was half worn-out when he got it, and it wasn't paid for. I guess it had been refinanced half a dozen times. It was a four-wheeled conglomeration of junk, wired together. It had to be cranked and was always contrary about starting.

On this day he was out there twisting on the crank, trying to get the engine to catch, and it wouldn't, and the day had been bad, and he was feeling punk, and suddenly it was too much for him and he needed to let off some steam.

"He pulled the crank out of the car," Ima Ruthie told me, "and started banging on the hood, beating it with the crank with all his might. Scared me half to death. You remember the radiator cap, that had the thermometer in it so you could tell how hot the radiator was? And it had two wings sticking out on either side, with knobs on the ends of them. Well, he raised the crank over his head, holding on to it with both hands like he was chopping wood, and he brought the crank down and knocked off one of those wings, and then he raised it again and knocked off the other one, and then he started going around the car, bamming on it with that crank. I thought he had gone crazy or something."

When he got through beating up the rear end and began on the right side, Ima Ruthie slumped in the seat, terrified. If he'd gone crazy, no telling what he'd do to her.

But he ran out of steam. He dropped the crank and reached in and patted my sister on the head, to show he was all right. He leaned against the car a few minutes, getting his wind

139 / HOME TOWN

back, collecting himself. He picked up the crank. He looked in and turned on an embarrassed little grin and said:

"Well, Ima Ruthie, let's see if that helped any."

He carefully fitted the crank in the hole and gave it two quick turns. The engine started and they went on.

He didn't mention that event at home, ever. We wondered why the radiator cap was mauled that way, and why the hood and the roof had all those dents, but we didn't ask. That extraordinary episode remained a secret for many years, between Ima Ruthie and our father.

Long after all these things happened, it became important to me to establish the low points of our Hard Times. I believe those points were different for each of us. For me, the low was two days before Christmas on that sheep ranch, when I thought I would never see my father again. Then when he returned, life for me began improving and went on from there and it has never been that low again.

I think my father's worst time was that first year in Eastland when he was out there peddling magazines, calling out "Need any help?" and pretending to be in high spirits, when he was ashamed to drive his own car across the courthouse square. And not really making any money, getting help from his daughter to support us. A daughter who should have been going to college, going to dances, having dates and fun.

I lay in bed and watched what I think was his darkest hour.

It came on a cold, cold morning. In these times, no meteorologist appeared to say that the temperature would sink below freezing during the night, so protect pipes and pets and tender vegetation. People went out and looked at the sky, and tested the air. Then they guessed how cold the night would be. According to that guess, they prepared.

On this night, my father guessed wrong and didn't drain the water out of the old Chevy's radiator. It froze tight, and the ice cracked the block of the engine.

I was recuperating from diphtheria and wasn't going to school. I heard him making a noise I was not familiar with. He had a large assortment of noises that I knew and I could tell this was his noise but I hadn't heard it before, didn't recognize it. I shifted to the edge of my bed so I could look in the back bedroom and see him.

He was crying.

He was an emotional person and I had seen him shed tears but I'd never heard him cry, sob out loud. A grown man crying, trying not to make noise, trying to muffle his weeping, makes exceptional sounds. I might make a passing job of describing them but I don't want to. They are painful to me. I have heard this a very few times, and the first time I heard the sounds they came from my own father and I've never had a more shattering experience.

I didn't want to watch him or listen to him but I did. He kicked off his shoes and took off his pants and got into bed and pulled the covers over his head. He couldn't stop sobbing. I believe I understood why. He had taken the ultimate blow. The other blows he had absorbed. But now, whatever it was fighting against him had taken away his great treasure—his wheels. There was no way he could afford a new engine or a major repair job on that old car.

My mother came and sat by him on the bed and patted him and spoke to him as if she were comforting a child. "There now, there now. Don't cry. It's all right. Things will be all right."

About this time I was walking to school and I found a leather pouch with drawstrings. I had seen such pouches in picture shows. I looked in and saw sparkling stones. They looked like gems. I took them downtown to the jewelry shop on the courthouse square. The man there examined them with a powerful magnifying glass and said at last, "Well, they're genuine, every one. They're worth a thousand dollars." A thousand! I took the money and went to the car company. A splendid new Chevy sat gleaming on the showroom floor. I asked the man how much. He said $800. I asked if it would start on cold mornings, and run. He said yes. I asked if it had to be cranked. He said no, that it had a thing *called a self-starter and he showed me how it worked. I said I'd take it. I gave him the $800 and drove the car home. I had never before driven a car but I was careful and had no trouble. I went into the room where my father was still in bed and said to him, "Come out, and see what I have for you." He came out and I handed him the keys to the new car. I had $200 left and I gave that to him, as well. He was really happy. That night we celebrated. The girls made candy—real fudge, with chocolate—and my father played his harmonica and patted his foot and Ima Ruthie led us in songs and everything was all right again.*

Uncle Barney came to visit us, and we went in the rabbit business.

Uncle Barney had something to do also with getting the car fixed. I don't know in what way, but it got fixed, and we began building rabbit hutches all over the back yard. We brought in a few pairs of New Zealand Reds and New Zealand Whites and before long we had rabbits everywhere.

They were soft and cute and cuddly and Ima Ruthie was delighted with them and gave them names. But her delight turned to dismay when she found out the rabbits were to be sold and slaughtered and eaten.

When the rabbits grew to eating size, sometimes people would come buy a few and my father would kill and dress them. Once he brought one in the house and my mother fried it for supper. We picked at the meat in a cautious way, kept reassuring each other that it was good, that it tasted a lot the same as chicken. But it was hard to enjoy eating rabbit with Ima Ruthie sobbing in the bathroom. We ate rabbit only that one time, and within a few weeks we passed out of the rabbit business.

The rabbits remind me that we held curious notions about what was civil and what was barbaric. To kill a rabbit you picked him up by the hind legs and held your free hand rigid and hit him a sharp blow just behind the ears with the edge of the hand. The old rabbit punch, familiar to wrestling fans.

My father didn't want me to watch that and would send me away when he began killing rabbits.

But I would sneak back and watch anyhow. I always wanted to see or hear what my parents said was not proper for me, because it was certain to be interesting and educational.

Compare the slaughter of a rabbit with that of a chicken. If my mother asked for a chicken to cook for Sunday, my father pulled one out of the coop on the back of the car and wrung its neck. I suppose many people now old enough to vote never saw a chicken gets it neck wrung. You grabbed it by the neck, picked it up that way, and rotated the neck fast, similar to cranking a car except the rotation was in a smaller circle. You had to rotate the neck faster than the body could follow so that pretty soon the head came off and the chicken dropped to the ground and jumped and flopped for a long while. It might flop all over the back yard.

My father, who thought the killing of a rabbit might be traumatic for a child, not only let me watch him wring a chicken's neck but tried to teach me how to do it. We would squat together and watch the headless chicken flop, and remark on how high it could jump without its head. Sometimes we'd put a washtub upside-down over the chicken and it would finish flopping beneath the tub. But this wasn't to hide an unpleasantness. It was to keep the poor bird from flopping back under the house where we couldn't get at it.

The rabbit business was a failure, and lost money. Uncle Barney shrugged it off. He came around frequently during the rabbit project. My guess is he had found a pretty good game about that time and financed the rabbits. When he came by he would often be in a nice car. The next time he came he might be on foot. He might be wearing a good overcoat one visit and then no coat at all the next. But he was always grinning and in a good humor, walking or riding.

Losing a few dollars on rabbits, if indeed he had any money in them at all, meant little to Uncle Barney. He just laughed and walked away.

■

For breakfast we sometimes ate what I came to think of as coal-oil hotcakes. Coal oil was kerosene. Hotcakes were what most people now call pancakes.

My mother cooked on a kerosene stove. A gallon jar of fuel sat in a rack at one end of the stove and was gravity-fed to the burners. In cold weather when the house had to be kept shut, we could smell kerosene in every room. Some of the food she fixed on that old stove actually tasted like kerosene. I got to a point where I didn't mind it. Which probably proves that I could have gotten accustomed to anything, if I could learn to like the combined taste of hotcakes, butter, molasses, and kerosene.

I'm not sure whether our diet, with its extraordinary features such as coal-oil hotcakes, had anything to do with the fact that we were often sick. I was forever having what we called bilious spells. Some years I had one every time the moon was full. The treatment for bilious spells was bed rest and laxatives.

Our mother was a relentless dispenser of purgatives. Calomel was the principal weapon in her arsenal. The minute you felt the least bit feverish or looked a shade pale, she would pronounce you bilious and bring out the calomel.

She might get short of sugar or flour in her kitchen but she was never short of patent medicines. The one I hated the least was syrup of pepsin. My mother used it only for mild cases. It didn't taste bad enough to suit her. When she wanted power, she depended on evil taste. Castor oil, or Epsom salts. I can look this very day at a castor bean plant growing in a flower bed and get nauseated.

I'm not saying our mother enjoyed spooning medicine down us but I think that's when she felt most useful, most in control. "There," she'd say, when the last of the castor oil had gone down, and stayed, "there now." In the most satisfied tone.

I wonder if she knew that the most effective medicine she ever gave us was the touch of her hand. She had marvelous hands. I don't know, maybe all mothers do. When I had a fever, she would come in the night and place her open hand on my forehead. Which was a way of testing for fever but she would leave her hand there a long time, much longer than necessary to check for fever. That hand had power. Its touch could soothe a churning stomach. Relieve a pain. Calm a fear. No medicine she poured out of a bottle could help a sick person the way her hand could.

If eating hotcakes flavored by kerosene is a recipe for biliousness, I don't care now. That old cookstove made for me the first money I ever saved.

It burned almost a gallon of fuel a day so at least six times a week I took a dime and a gallon can and walked over the hill and down to Commerce Street, where a gas station sold kerosene. It cost nine cents a gallon. I was allowed to keep the penny change.

This was a little lesson my mother was giving me, on how the accumulation of money comes about. Six cents a week. Twenty-four cents a month. I started dropping a penny a day into a pint fruit jar. That seemed mighty tedious to me. In a week I walked six round trips to the station and dropped six pennies in the jar and I couldn't tell the level of coppers had got any higher than when I began. So my mother showed me a system of saving pennies that provided more satisfaction.

She handed me a small glass, just a tiny thing. I think of it now as the size of a whiskey shot glass, although that image would be an abomination to my mother. She told me to drop the daily penny in that little glass. It would take less than two weeks to get it full. Then pour the full glass of pennies into the pint jar and I would actually see the level climb, rising before my eyes.

This is a significant clue to the character of the woman, and women like her who endured the adversity of the period. Don't look closely at the broad picture of the future because the wide view is bleak, the goal too distant. But giving up hope is unthinkable so you take things one step at a time, and among the negatives you search for positives. Every day you find at least one positive, one penny dropping into the tiny glass. You save these, let them accumulate, and at the end of a week, a month, a year, you look at the whole of them and you see that they are significant and good and you say, "Why, see here, progress is being made. The level is rising."

This view of things was reflected in her daily work, so much of which was tedious.

My mother and I often spent entire days and evenings together, when the others were gone or involved in their private doings. We would always work. At night we would often shell peas. We would sit in the kitchen and shell a bushel of black-eyes or purple hulls between supper and bedtime.

She didn't like to shell peas into a big pot. Took too long to fill it. You could shell for an hour and you'd have the bottom of a big pot covered and that's about all. Not enough progress to be satisfying. So she would shell into a small vessel not much bigger than a cup. She could fill it in a few minutes and then she'd pour the small pot into the big one and it meant something. It made the level rise.

I believe she spent all her life doing that, sustaining her spirit on occasional surges of gratification.

We had that old stove about two years. In that time I filled the fruit jar with pennies. This pleased my mother as much as anything I'd ever done. She'd say, "Pretty soon you'll have enough to open a savings account, and let those pennies grow to you."

Before I took the pennies to the bank I had to wash them, because they all smelled like kerosene.

We didn't stop moving. But instead of moving from one town to another, we moved from one house to another in the same town. From the orange house we moved over on West Main, which is the same as U.S. Highway 80 going through town. The rent must have been mighty low because we didn't have to make any kind of deal. My mother didn't have to cook for anybody but us. We were in an entire house, all alone, five of us. It seemed strange.

In little towns like Eastland you could live inside the city limits and still be almost in the country. On West Main we had neighboring houses next door and across the street, and cars going by all the time on the highway in front. But behind the house was the country. The land rose up gradually and became woods. Scrub oak and mesquite and briar patches. Also native bluestem grass, which my father looked on with favor. "Pretty good grazing," he said.

So he got another milk cow.

He loved to milk, and was easy to please about a place to live if there was room in the back to keep a cow. I think going out and fooling with a cow was a pleasant diversion for him. Not for me. I was not overjoyed to see that new cow. What would happen is, my father would bring in a cow and get her settled, as he said. Then he'd jump in the old Chevy and leave town and I'd have the cow to milk and look after.

The looking after was more bother than the milking. It involved a process called staking. This meant leading the cow around town in search of a vacant lot where you could tie her to graze. If there was no tree or fence post to tie her to, you carried a stake and a hammer and drove the stake down and tied to that. Then you had to go get the cow two or three times a day and bring her in to water, and take her back out again to a fresh place.

Fooling with a cow that way was a pain to me because I was beginning to have an interest in socializing. One Saturday I was walking along a dirt street on the north side of town, carrying my hammer, going back home from staking the cow, and I saw this girl come out of a house. She walked almost out to the street and picked up a kitten. Her name was Elsie, a new girl whose folks had just moved to town. She looked at me and said, "You're in Mrs. Tucker's room at school and I am too." She went back in the house and said no more but I counted her statement a regular love song.

It was uncomfortable, being in love so much. I liked it but it hurt. At school I needed to look at Elsie frequently but I certainly didn't want her to catch me at it. She was a darter, though, and quicker than I was. When she would turn and see me looking, I would pretend I was interested in an arithmetic problem on the blackboard just behind her. Never in all my life did I see on a blackboard or anywhere else an arithmetic problem that interested me, but being in love that way required a lot of acting.

The place I most enjoyed being with Elsie was the picture show on Saturday afternoons. The Lyric Theater had a wonderful deal for kids. For a dime you could see a cowboy movie that began about 1 P.M. Ima Ruthie and I would collect wire coat hangers and sell them at Modern Dry Cleaners for enough to see the show. It would be a fine horse opera starring Buck Jones or Tim McCoy or Hoot Gibson or Tom Keene. In addition to the feature you would get a cartoon—Krazy Kat, probably, or one of the early Mickey Mouse features.

What I liked best were the serials. Continued pieces, as we sometimes called them. They were not always westerns. Some were Hoodlums versus Good Guys. Railroad stories were popular then. Hoodlums would spend thirty minutes every Saturday afternoon, for ten or twelve weeks, trying to take over a railroad from the Good Guys on the screen of the Lyric.

The Main Good Guy was always on top of a speeding train at the end of each episode, and the locomotive would explode and kill him. So he was dead, but he *wasn't* dead, and we knew it because this was only Chapter Six. All week long we would argue about how the Good Guy saved himself. He did it by leaping from the train at the last second and catching onto the limb of a tree that couldn't have been there, but was. This was splendid stuff. We loved impossibilities.

Most of the youngsters in that town, from fourth graders to high school students, would stay all afternoon in the Lyric. We would see the same show four or five times until we could voice the dialogue along with the figures on the screen. The usher would let us go out between shows and use the toilets across the street in the courthouse and go back in the theater without paying another dime.

The Lyric was an excellent place for me to look at Elsie when she didn't know it. Evidently she had weak eyes because she always sat down near the front. This was an advantage for me. I could go in and sit somewhere in the middle and I knew she was in front of me somewhere. When my eyes grew accustomed to the darkness and I was able to spot her, I would start moving closer. One row at a time.

Before the first show was over, I might be within two rows of her. I might hear a thing she said, see her hand go up to scratch her ear, hear the rustle of her dress when she moved. But I never got closer than that.

So being in love with Elsie was mostly a matter of looking at her. She didn't look at me very often but when she did, I certainly didn't like for her to see me leading a milk cow down the middle of the street.

The summer on West Main was a good one for my father. He not only got his milk cow. He shed his chicken coop and went back on the road, selling those package-sealing machines. He traveled far, and came home telling of wonderful places. This is when my world began to expand.

It needed expansion in a desperate way. The proof of that is, I thought it was already big. It stretched from Fort Worth on the east all the way across Eastland County, a hundred miles or more. Southward it reached fifty miles, from Highway 80 down to Hico in Hamilton County. So by the time I finished the sixth grade, I was living in a world shaped like an inverted triangle enclosing five entire Texas counties and parts of three others. I knew of places outside the triangle, like Houston, and Dallas, but I had never been to them and didn't think I ever would.

My father came home talking of such places as Lubbock, Amarillo, Nacogdoches, Wichita Falls, Odessa, Harlingen, Kingsville. He knew what the road looked like between Sonora and Eldorado, between Pampa and Borger. We would be driving to Grandma's Farm for a Sunday afternoon visit and come to a stretch of country that wasn't characteristic of our immediate world and he would say, "This looks like the road between Cuero and Yoakum." He loved roads and how they looked.

He began to bring interesting things home from his travels. Silhouette cards. A white card with a black profile of, say, a human figure with a white speck in the middle. You stared thirty seconds at the speck, closed your eyes, and behold, the image of the human figure was captured inside your closed eyes. A marvelous thing.

He brought two wild turkey eggs from out close to Uvalde. The antler of a white-tailed deer from the Big Thicket in East Texas. Two eggplants, dark purple shiny beauties. We had never seen any, no more than we'd seen an artichoke or a rutabaga or a Brussels sprout. Another time he came in with a quart jar of fresh goat's milk. We poured it over our cereal and ate it before he told us what it was. It was fine before he told us. Afterward we thought it smelled bad. My mother, always ready with a gem of medical knowledge, said goat's milk was good for the stomach, that Dr. Oxford used to prescribe it for people with stomach ulcers.

As a consequence of that remark, my father brought home from his next trip a pair of Spanish milk goats.

I see him now, turning in off the highway, laughing behind the windshield. Laughing because the goats were standing in the back seat of the car with their heads poked out of the open windows.

For a while the goats were an entertainment but now we had three things that had to be milked. Actually the goats were not so much trouble to milk. You put a little feed in an elevated trough and the goat would hop onto a box and eat and you could sit on a low stool and milk her comfortably. If she wasn't elevated she was way too low to the ground. You would need almost to lie down to get at her udder.

But those goats made trouble for me.

One of my chores was to keep them off the beds. This curious duty came about because all of us slept outdoors that summer, in the back yard. In West Texas that was not uncommon. That part of the state was dry and didn't produce enough mosquitoes to carry entire families off, and so many of us slept in the yard because it was too blamed hot in the house.

A couple of days after the goats came, my sister Maifred looked out in the back yard and both those creatures were asleep, each in the center of a double bed, as if the beds had been put out there for their comfort.

Occasionally there comes into this world a Spanish goat that is peeved, as a general condition. Whitey was such a goat. She was half the pair my father brought home. She could pretend sometimes to be a nice goat but she was not nice. She was only setting you up. You could leave her nodding drowsily in the back yard and ten minutes later she would be wide awake and eating the sleeve off a shirt on the clothesline.

She found joy in butting. She would butt anything, even the front fender of my father's Chevy. She butted dogs, the bigger the better. Bushel baskets. Fences and their posts. Beds and their steads. She also butted butts. Butts were her favorite target. Not a minute after I had fed her one afternoon, Whitey thanked me by lowering her head and lunging and getting me square in the seat of my overalls and making me a temporary cripple. I did not love that goat.

But I learned from her an important thing. It had to do with telling the truth. The lesson was that the truth is not always the right thing to tell. My mother said it was but Whitey showed me it wasn't.

When she would get loose—which she could do any time she cared to—she would roam around town doing damage. I was the one who had to go find her. I had the hope that I would *not* find her, that maybe I would never see her again. But she was always easily found. I just went looking for trouble and when I came across it, there Whitey would be in the middle of it.

She loved flowers. Irises. Lilies. Roses. Larkspurs. Nasturtiums. She loved the same flowers that particular homemakers loved. The usual circumstance was, a lady would be out on her front porch waving a broom and yelling, "Shoo! Shoo!" and Whitey would be standing in the flower bed, not paying any attention, finishing off a row of violets.

The lady would say to me, "Do you know who this animal belongs to?"

I perfected an answer to that. It was, "No ma'am, but if you want me to I can take her away and try to find out whose she is."

What I'm a little smug about now is that not a one of those ladies ever heard anything suspicious in that reply. They were too relieved to find somebody willing to lead the goat off their property. In fact, most of them expressed their appreciation, and thanked me, and said silently that I was a good boy, doing kindnesses for ladies.

That was the valuable teaching I received from a Spanish goat.

Another lesson I received around this time was about politics. It came from my parents and it was short and simple. My parents seemed to be telling me that this one lesson covered all I'd ever need to know about national affairs. It came in two parts.

Part One: President Herbert Hoover had caused the Depression and had led us to the brink of extinction. Part Two: Franklin Roosevelt was our savior, descended out of heaven to land in the state of New York, from whence he would come to deliver us into prosperity everlasting, amen.

I never heard anybody pray to Roosevelt but for a while there I thought we were all about to start. Many houses I went into had pictures of Jesus Christ and FDR hanging side by side. We had a picture of Roosevelt but none of Jesus. My mother was not comfortable with pictures of Jesus on the living-room wallpaper.

I'm pretty sure this was because she thought it was too much like something the Catholics did, with their beads and their little statues. My mother never said anything against the Catholics but you could see her straining to keep from it.

They were good people, sure, and God loved them the same as he loved everybody but, after all, they weren't exactly the same as Methodists, now, were they?

The first Inner Struggle I was aware of in the Methodist Church occurred when our choir wanted to wear white robes. My mother and many of the other Methodist mothers were against white robes because they looked Catholic. The choir finally got its robes but I don't believe the anti-Catholic mothers ever got accustomed to them.

Very few Catholics lived in our little town. They had a small frame church on the south side. The word was passed around among children that the priest in that church was the Devil. This idea caused me to have a great interest in him. It wasn't every day you could see the Devil strolling along the street.

Once I was in a bunch of kids kicking a football on a vacant lot. The ball bounced into the street just when that priest was walking past. I ran after it but he took it neatly on the bounce before I could get to it. He hid the ball on his hip, like a tailback faking a run. He looked at me and said, "OK, short pass over the middle. Five yards and cut left."

Any boy in town knew what that meant. I ran the five yards and cut sharp to the left. He had faded back a little and let go a nice pass, arching just right, leading me perfectly. My own mother could have caught it. He went on then and didn't look back. We watched him go. How could a Catholic priest know to do such a thing?

Later, on the way home, I thought of a way I could make a pretty nice impression at supper. I could say, "I sure caught a good pass today."

"Who threw it?" they would ask.

"The Devil," I would answer. But I decided I'd better not mention it, and I didn't.

After we'd been in Eastland a couple of years, we were well settled in matters of religion and politics. We'd all joined the First Methodist Church, FDR was in the White House, and Ima Ruthie's Sunday School record was smooth and unbroken.

From West Main we moved a little way over onto Commerce Street, into an apartment building. My father had found another deal and my mother went back to cooking for other people.

The building was owned by a Mrs. Pierce. She had two teen-aged children and she ran a beauty shop. Her hair was dyed. We had never lived under the same roof with anybody with dyed hair and we talked about it before we moved in. My mother decided it was all right. At times she could be broad-minded.

Four apartments were in that building, two up and two down. The Pierces lived in one of the lower apartments and we lived in the other. For the rent, my mother fed the Pierces. Three times a day they would come over and eat with us. I remember what my mother said after the first three meals.

"They won't be very hard to please, but my, my, that boy. He'll be hard to fill up."

She meant Ray Pierce. He was a couple of years older than I was but about twice as big. He was a good-natured boy with the appetite of an ox. We would sit in a state of wonder and watch him eat. It was my mother's custom at breakfast to put out a little pitcher of pure cream for the oatmeal, so that each person could have just a bit. The first breakfast Ray was with us, the cream pitcher was put down in front of his plate. He emptied it on his oatmeal, thinking it was all meant for him. He thought everything was for him. He poured milk in a way that I had never seen before, and haven't since. He watched the pitcher he was pouring out of, rather than the glass he was pouring into. We decided he did it this way so he could be certain he was getting all the milk out of the pitcher, even if it meant overflowing his glass.

Ray gained weight while we lived in that apartment building, and became a good friend for me. He made model airplanes and had a crystal set, the first radio I ever listened to. We took turns with the headsets, straining to hear the Light Crust Doughboys out of Fort Worth. And we heard Dr. Brinkley, one of the nation's early electronic medical evangelists, broadcasting out of Del Rio, hawking his goat-gland implantations that were said to restore the manhood of aging but eager gents.

Mrs. Pierce was either a widow or a divorcee, I forget which. Anyway she didn't have a husband when we moved into her building. Before we moved out, she got one. Got him by mail out of Florida. She had set up a correspondence with him through some sort of lonely hearts club. She would talk about it at the dinner table and we were all very good about listening. One day she announced he was coming and they were going to get married, even though they had never met.

This match-by-mail proposition surely improved the general interest in life around that apartment house. We counted the days the same as Mrs. Pierce did. We were as nervous as she was about the meeting. Wouldn't it be awful if they hated one another on sight? Everybody in the neighborhood knew in advance about his arrival. Our yard was full of kids pretending to play, when they were just hanging around to watch Mrs. Pierce meet her fiancé. The adults were watching, as well, but not openly. They were all standing inside, close by windows so they could peek out.

We had never seen a person from Florida and I couldn't get out of my head the notion that he would look strange, like a man from a foreign country. Maybe like a Chinese. Actually he looked like an ordinary middle-aged gent with a good round beaming face. He was about half the size of Ray, who met him in the yard and shook his hand.

I supposed there would be a great awkwardness in the meeting between this little man and Mrs. Pierce. It was not so. No attempt was made to keep the meeting private. They rushed to one another and embraced on the front porch. There was much laughing and hugging, and re-hugging, and re-laughing. This became for us all an emotional event. Two people who would be married the next day, meeting for the first time. I now feel privileged to have been a witness.

When the couple went into the house, Ray turned to me and held out the hand his mother's fiancé had just shaken. He said, "He's sure got a grip on him."

After she was married, Mrs. Pierce sold the apartment building and the family moved to Florida. We never saw them again.

In summer we would go back to Grandma's Farm for special gatherings, such as the Fourth of July when kinfolks from all around would convene. My father's morale continued to mend. He got a new harmonica, which we never called by that name. We called it a French harp. He would play tunes on it while we rolled down the highway, going to Grandma's.

We counted ourselves city people again, the same as when we lived in Fort Worth. We might have a milk cow and two Spanish goats in the back yard but we didn't consider ourselves rural, despite that we did a lot of mighty rural things.

For example, on the way to Grandma's we would stop at an icehouse and buy two 50-pound blocks for freezing home-made ice cream. Most people, carrying ice a long distance on a hot day, wrapped it in burlap to keep it from melting. But my father put it on the front bumpers of the Chevy. A hundred pounds of ice was a status symbol. The bumpers of that old car were just narrow strips of metal bolted onto brackets so they made handy racks where the ice could ride for the public to see.

My father didn't mind arriving a little later than all the others, so we'd have a satisfactory audience. Half a mile before we got to Grandma's, he would stop and Ima Ruthie and I would get out and sit on the front fenders. To keep from falling off we'd throw a leg over a headlight, which was round and the size of a volley ball, and we'd hold onto what was left of the radiator cap after our father had mauled it that time.

I can't imagine anything more cornball than the way we

would go roaring up the lane to the house, where the audience waited on the front porch, my father waving his hat out the window and honk-honk-honking the horn. Here we come, folks, get ready for us. Ima Ruthie and I riding on the fenders, slinging our arms around like bronc riders, our bare feet propped on the melting ice, and we'd be singing loud as we could, "She'll be comin' around the mountain when she comes!"

Sure, it was a joke, but a serious one. It was Fred Hale and his gang arriving from the city in style. The kinfolks laughed at us and we laughed too but mainly because we thought it was a pretty neat arrival, putting on a show that way.

My father liked to take to these gatherings a contribution that would make everybody exclaim. He would do the same at home. Those goats, for instance. I still think one of the reasons he bought them was that he could anticipate going home with the head of a live goat poking out of his car windows on each side. Once when we went to the farm he took a full stalk of bananas and hung it on the porch, the way bananas were displayed then in grocery stores. The women would see that and shriek. "WHERE in the WORLD'd all those buh-NAN-uhs come from?" That's what he wanted to hear. Then the answer to the question, which he wanted to hear even more, would be, "Well, Fred brought 'em. Where do you THINK they came from?"

Shortly before we moved out of the apartment building, two good things happened. The first was that my father brought home the biggest surprise he had ever brought—a new car.

It was not new in the way cars are new now. It was new only to us. It was four years old and had a bad clutch and 50,000 miles on it. It was a four-door Willys-Knight sedan. I went around the neighborhood telling people about our new car and they came and kicked the tires as if it were sitting on a showroom floor. My father would travel in this sedan for the next four years.

The other good thing that happened was the dog. One day I was crossing West Main on my way to the grocery store and this large dog, with curly coat and curious brown and black markings, came wagging up to me. I patted his head and went on to the store.

When I came out he was waiting for me. From that day on, until I finished school, that old dog was waiting for me when I came out of almost any door. We named him Jiggs. He turned out to be a great lover and left his wavy hair and brown and black colors on many puppies all around town. When he wasn't courting, he went where I went, the same as Red Dog in Glen Rose.

We never learned where he came from. Probably he had been left behind by a family passing through on the highway. He had been loved and cared for. He was not a country dog. When we roamed across pastures and along creeks, he did not understand how to deal with things like grass burs. He didn't know how to bite them out of his pads with his teeth, the way other dogs did. He would stand in a grass bur patch with stickers in all four paws and just look pitiful. I often had to carry him out of sticker patches, which was a chore because he weighed about eighty pounds. He did not know how to swim. Dog people would laugh at that and say all dumb creatures know how to swim at birth, even chickens, but this dog did not. He almost drowned one day trying to follow me across a creek. I taught him to swim. Old Jiggs. He improved my life.

Close Shave

WE WERE PLAYING CISCO, *our favorite football team to hate. We had never won over Cisco, ever. We thought that they cheated, and that's why we couldn't beat them. They weren't as bad about cheating as Ranger but they were bad. Ranger was shameless. We had been told they had men on their high school football team who were twenty-five years old, and we believed this. We believed also that their fullback was married and had three children and one of them was already in the pep squad. We believed that was why we couldn't beat Ranger, the same as we couldn't beat Cisco. On this day I was playing halfback on defense. I weighed 112 pounds. Cisco was leading 6–0 with only a few seconds left in the game. They had the ball on our 10-yard line and were trying to score again before time ran out. Their quarterback then pulled a boner. He threw a little pass to his halfback out in the right flat. I couldn't believe what a nice thing that was for me, because I could see in advance that I would be able to intercept that pass. I came charging up at full throttle, plucked the ball out of the hands of the receiver, and sped ninety yards for a touchdown as the final gun sounded. Then I drop-kicked the extra point and split the uprights squarely. So we won 7–6. I was carried off the field by my teammates. My name was on the lips of all the pretty girls, even the cheerleaders. That night I got a phone call from the mayor. I was given an A in algebra.*

The year we beat Cisco for the first time, I was in the band.

When I got up in junior high I told my mother it was clear that I would never amount to anything in that school unless I played football. I told her a student could be president of his class, make straight A's, become captain of the debate team and graduate valedictorian, and he would not amount to as much in that school as a second-string guard on the football team. I said this because I thought it was true.

My mother said playing football was too dangerous for me. Remember what the doctor had said—no licks on the head. I said yes but in football they wore these thick helmets and getting hit on the head didn't hurt. Besides, I said, I had gotten lots of licks on the head since that operation and nothing happened except a few knots rose up.

Finally my mother relented and I went out for football in the seventh grade. Actually we didn't wear thick helmets. We didn't wear helmets at all. We used the equipment that the varsity had worn out. We had pants way too big for us. We had jerseys that were ragged. We had no cleats. I played in the same tennis shoes I wore to school.

One day we went up to Breckenridge to play the junior high team there. I was trying to tackle a guy and I fell and hit the side of my head on Jack Bagley's knee. Jack was in on the tackle. He was on our side and didn't mean for my head to hit his knee but it did and with a terrific bell-ringing force. That night I had the grandfather of all headaches and the entire right side of my face was swelled up something fierce. It stayed that way many days and in fact never did return entirely to its normal state.

Not a week later, on the schoolground, I got hit in the center of the forehead by a top. Yes, a wooden top, the kind that boys wrap a cord around and throw down and spin. Which sounds like a mild pursuit but playing tops could be a savage competition. The big boys would file their spindles down to the sharpness of a needle and try to plug the tops of their opponents and split them down the middle. So the tops were flung down with all the might of the flinger. If the cord happened to tangle around the spindle, the top would jerk back sharply and become a dangerous missile. Which is what hit me on the forehead and raised a great lump. It looked like a hen egg half-buried in the front of my skull, and it didn't go away.

My mother would take me to the doctor and ask, "What is the reason for this?" The doctor would shrug, and tell me not to play football or get hit in the head anymore. I joined the band.

In junior high school my class got an assignment to write a theme about a subject of the writer's choice. I wrote about the same old thing, the house catching fire in Stamford. I had been writing about it in themes several years by then and had it down pretty well.

The teacher gave all those papers to a judge who was looking for compositions to enter into a statewide contest. I was amazed when I won third place. Not in the statewide contest but only in the preliminaries, third place in my class only. I had never come out as high as third in a contest of any sort and I became thoughtful. Was it possible I had a talent for telling stories on paper?

I was curious about the themes that placed higher than mine. The teacher let me read the first-place paper. It was about a boy who had been shipwrecked and was bobbing around in the ocean off a desert island, and how he saved himself. I remember the last line in the piece. It was wonderful:

"I quickly took a bar of soap and washed myself ashore."

That one sentence caused me to abandon the notion that I could ever be any good at writing stories. I would never be able to think up a line half as clever as that.

The year I was a freshman in high school, I had what we liked to call a very close shave. I have never told this but I am telling everything else so I might as well record the close shave. It became extremely important to me.

I had borrowed a .22 rifle and was hunting down south of

town, alone. Normally when hunting I would be with my friend Dude Wilkins but he had gotten a Saturday job and was working. The gun belonged to him or probably to his older brother. My family had no gun of any sort. My father had a rifle before the Depression struck but it went into that warehouse in Fort Worth with the furniture and was lost.

In a pasture not far outside the city limits we had seen a couple of squirrels in a little grove of oaks and that's where I headed. But not directly. We never went anywhere directly then. There was time, time, time, and an entire world of woods and fields and creeks to roam in, and the future looked really good to me. Dude and I had made some long-range plans. When we got a couple of years older and earned some money and bought us our own rifle and shotgun, maybe we would go up on the Clear Fork of the Brazos and spend the whole summer, hunting and fishing and swimming. From there, no telling where we might go. We might build a boat and float the river. It could be done. We traced it out on a map. We could float all the way to the Gulf. And then what? Maybe get a job on a ship, see the world. Such beautiful dreams. The morning I went into the pasture with Dude's little rifle, I was feeling really good about my life, and the future. The morning was sweet and warm. I wanted to sing, or laugh, or shout.

I think I did laugh a little when I got to Lyerla's tank. This was a stock watering tank with an earthen dam, and one of two popular swimming holes not far from our school. The other was Davenport's tank. No girls ever came near those tanks in hot weather because they would be full of naked boys, swimming.

This is why I laughed, thinking of a scene I had witnessed about a week earlier there at Lyerla's tank. Two naked boys, about sixteen and already the size of adults, fighting, and serious about it, too. They had an audience of maybe thirty other boys, standing around in a loose circle, and not a boy in the bunch had a thread of clothes on. Such a ridiculous sight.

Amateur fighters always look so awkward, even with their clothes on. But two amateurs fighting naked are a great farce, with all their moving parts waving and thrashing. Arms, legs, hands, feet, hair, elbows, penises, testicles, all flailing at once.

So even at this early stage of my time, I had seen some spectacles. And I had learned a thing or two that not every-body knew. There at those swimming holes, for example, I had found out what a bank walker is. He was the boy who was proud of his equipment and wanted to parade nude along the bank and show it off. He seldom went in the water. The non-bank walkers stayed out in the tank and stood in water about waist deep, waiting, hoping for more impressive credentials.

We hunted almost anything then. I circled Lyerla's a couple of times, and then Davenport's, hoping for a mudhen or a big cottonmouth moccasin or a turtle, if I saw one big enough to waste a .22 shell on. I went on into the mesquite pasture below Davenport's and eased up on the little mott of oaks where we'd seen the squirrels. Those oaks grew around a cluster of good-sized rocks, some high as my head. I got in among the rocks and took a seat and waited.

Still-hunting, we called it. You didn't go stomping around trying to flush a squirrel. You went where you knew squirrels were, and sat in silence. We killed a lot of squirrels that way.

When the squirrel showed himself, I couldn't get a clear shot at him. I stood, crouched, and began a step to the right, and slipped and fell. The rifle got away from me. I landed on my side, on solid rock. Just as I hit I heard the crack of the .22 firing and heard the bullet rip through the foliage of the oaks. The fall didn't hurt me much but I needed a second to get my breath back and let my eyes blink a time or two. When I could see again, what I saw was the muzzle of that little rifle, not a foot from my nose, and pointed straight between my eyes.

Evidently when the rifle fell on the rocks the impact caused it to fire. I would devote a lot of thought, many days there-after, to how far that bullet missed my head. It couldn't have been more than an inch. The slightest change of position, of the rifle or my head, could have put that bullet into my skull, and they would have found me there the next day.

That private event, between me and a gun, became an influence in my life. It changed me. It made me aware of my mortality, the tiny thread that kept me attached to the life I was just then beginning to love, and to the future that looked so exciting and good. I picked up the rifle and went on home, and that afternoon I didn't even go to the cowboy movie. My mother thought I was sick, and wanted to give me a laxative.

During the year after the gun episode, I amazed myself by growing about six inches. I also lost some of my interest in hunting because I took up serious sex on a full-time basis.

What I mean, I *thought* about it in a serious way, at least fourteen hours a day and half of most nights. I had known about sex for several years but I hadn't dreamed it would require so much attention. Suddenly it became a steady job. I didn't have time to think of anything else. How could they expect me to do two hours of homework every night, and concentrate on history and algebra? I couldn't fit history or algebra into my schedule. It was already overloaded with fantasies about girls.

One afternoon a friend whispered to me in the hall at school, "Go look in the crapper stall in the first-floor restroom."

I went straight there and looked. Above the toilet this sentence was scrawled:

"I fucked [name deleted] three times under the football stadium."

I wouldn't dare print the name of the girl but she was one of the prettiest in the entire school, and the smartest, and the most proper. Which is why her name appeared in the sentence. I would bet a forty-dollar bill that at her wedding she walked out of the church a virgin, purebred and registered. Never mind that. I could still see her under the stadium— probably with one of the football players—getting done to her what the sentence said, and liking it better the second time than she did the first, and the third time better yet. I re-membered Edgar, in the restroom at George Clarke School in Fort Worth, and how he had put it to all the pretty girls by the railroad track, and made them howl. I wondered if (name deleted) howled, there beneath the stadium seats. I decided she did.

Nobody believed the scrawler of that sentence had told the truth but that didn't make the statement less effective. The ap-pearance of the girl's name, as the object of that forbidden but wallop-packing verb, was a shocker. A dozen of us crowded in front of the toilet stall to study the sentence. Somebody could have charged admission. When one dozen left, another dozen came in to take their places. The idea of (name deleted) getting it put to her that way made my face hot, my legs weak, my insides churn—the same symptoms I'd felt in the packing crate long ago in Stamford when that little girl said, "There it is."

There were things about sex I didn't like. It interfered with all the activities I'd enjoyed before I entered into it full-time. I couldn't even fish. I could take Old Jiggs and go to a fine little perch-and-catfish hole I knew below the Eastland Lake Dam on the Leon River. While I lay there on the bank, staring up into the trees and seeing among the leaves nothing but naked girls, the fish would strip my bait off the hook and I never knew I was getting a bite.

They would come to me in the night. Two of them, sometimes three at once, the most beautiful girls in school. I had seen slow-motion at the picture show and that's how they would come, walking in dreamy ways, with crooked knowing smiles and half-closed eyes. They dressed in flimsy gowns or pink underwear or sometimes in long fur coats that swung open and showed they wore nothing underneath. They would come to my bed and look down, smiling, and their gowns and underwear and coats, what-ever they wore, would come off and they would say to me, "There it is." They would take my hands and pull me out of my bed and we would go running off across strange green meadows that I had never seen before, and through enchanted woods, touching and laughing, and any time we wanted to we would stop in soft places and do wonderful and wicked things.

I had reached a point where I could go up and talk to girls without very much stammering but what I needed to do was touch one. As far as I knew, you weren't allowed to touch one. At last I discovered a sneaky way to do it. The first time was an accident.

Between classes at school, the hallways were extremely crowded. Hundreds of students going along shoulder to shoulder, carrying books, going to lockers, turning sideways sometimes to keep from running into one another. One morning in this heavy traffic I made the sideways turn and the back of my hand brushed across a girl's behind. A be*hind!* It was the best thing I had ever felt, and I was staggered. I had hoped to touch a hand, an arm, an elbow, a shoulder. But a behind was far more than I had hoped for. The remainder of that day, while I was supposed to be getting educated, I sat in class and thought of nothing but the smooth wonder of that girl's seat.

At the beginning of my sophomore year, my classmates and I were introduced to what I considered a fantastic social activity. The introduction was made by our parents and the school administrators. I could scarcely believe it.

I am talking about ballroom dancing.

Up to this time, most of the rules set forth by our adults were intended to keep boys and girls separated. Then suddenly they said, "All right, we're going to have dances in the gym."

To me, about to turn sixteen, dancing was indiscriminant, unbridled sex.

On the dance floor you not only got to hold a girl's hand, you got to put your arm around her. You got to *feel* her. You could feel the exquisite inward curve at her waist, the delightful tapers and mysterious slopes of her. Few of us knew how to dance and that just made it better, more exciting, because we were forever bumping into and glancing off one another. "Excuse me, I'm sorry." I was not sorry. During one of those bumps you could feel knees, thighs, breasts, stomachs. Sometimes I would need to go sit down and calm myself, from all that bumping.

You needn't think I was unique. At those early dances, groups of boys would often stand outside the gym in the cool air and grin and wait until they got control of themselves. Then we would go back in for more.

A few of my contemporaries were having dates on a regular basis but the trouble was, something impossible had been added to the process of dating. That was the automobile. Several of the boys in my bunch had learned to drive and could borrow the family car for dates and this became a social requirement. We were emerging from the Depression and nobody wanted to look poor any longer. We were tired of poor. So nobody had a date unless they had a car or at least a ride.

I had a problem learning to drive. Sometimes my mother would give me a lesson in the Willys-Knight. She wasn't too good a driver but she wasn't a bad teacher. At least she had patience. My father had none. It made him so nervous for me to drive that he would grab the steering wheel or stomp the brake from the passenger side of the front seat.

One day he was downtown without the car and when my mother went to get him she let me drive. I had driven around town a little with her and hadn't hit anything important so when we got to where my father was, my mother suggested he get in the back and let me drive on home. She said it would give me confidence.

It didn't give *him* confidence, though. I could feel the way he was sitting, leaning forward with both hands gripping the back of the front seat. I could feel him breathing on me. I was going along probably at fifteen miles an hour and a car began backing out of a driveway into my path. Instead of stopping as I should have, I whipped the steering wheel to the right, and back then to the left, and made a tight little semicircle around that car and I must have missed it two or three inches.

I had never heard my father shout so loud. He yelled, "GOD DAMN!"

This outburst made a deep impression on me. My father never used such language in front of his family, and now I had provoked him to utter blasphemy. When we got home I promised myself I would never again drive when he was in the car, and for many years I did not.

Staying out of the car when he was in it wasn't very difficult, since most of the time he was gone, to places like Amarillo and Lubbock and Wichita Falls. My mother and my sisters and I never counted on having transportation. We always expected to walk wherever we needed to go, and most often did. To school, to work, to church, to the store, everywhere, in rain, shine, snow, or sleet. So I didn't really have formal dates until I was a senior.

But there were ways you could be around girls without having dates or cars.

Basketball games, for example. Basketball became my favorite sport and I seldom missed a game because if a girl came to the gymnasium on foot, she might let you walk home with her. This is the way I first kissed a girl, walking home after a basketball game. I was getting pretty tall by then and she was a short girl and the light was bad and I kissed her sort of high and to the right. But it was a kiss, I'm certain, because I asked her if we ought to try it again and she said no, that was enough.

Something like forty years later I saw this girl at a homecoming and I confessed to her that she was the first girl I ever kissed. She said she suspected it.

My parents had no idea I was indulging in all that sex. My mother seemed especially ignorant of what was happening.

One day I had been fishing with some of my gang and we had pretty good luck and I brought home a nice string of catfish and bream. I asked my mother to cook them. She agreed and even went out in the back yard to help me clean my catch.

Some of the bream had eggs in them and my mother saw those eggs as an opportunity to give me a lesson in the process of reproduction, just as if I had never thought of where babies came from.

She explained to me how fish performed the sex act, how the mother fish deposited her eggs in a sort of nest, under water. Then the father fish came along and fertilized those eggs which later hatched and out came baby fish. I thought I saw where she was headed with the lesson. I supposed she would follow up then and say something like, "Now, in the case of humans, the egg is inside the mother, just as these eggs are inside the fish, but the human father must find a way to fertilize the egg while it's still inside. Therefore, he performs what we call . . ." And so on and so forth.

She said no such thing. She ended the lecture, just as soon as the father fish got his job done over the nest. Either she lost her nerve, or she expected me to take the fish story and deduct from it the entire system of human reproduction. I think fish sex was more comfortable for her than the human kind because it involved no penetration.

Here was a woman, a doctor's daughter with the reputation of knowing more about medicine and biology than the average Texas mother, telling her sixteen-year-old son about the birds and bees without any mention of sexual intercourse. That may reflect one of the most extraordinary conditions of my time.

While she was talking to me about fish eggs and underwater nests, not fifty feet from us stood our Jersey cow with a new calf. A year earlier I had led that cow to a bull to be bred. I had stayed there to watch, according to my father's orders, to be certain she had been thoroughly accommodated. I had watched the calf being born in our back yard. I had disposed of the afterbirth, also according to the orders of my father, who was in Fort Stockton, or maybe it was Lamesa, or Rotan.

My mother was aware of all this and yet she pretended that I knew nothing of human biology. I suppose she found a comfort in that pretension. I am glad now she didn't know that, at sixteen, I was lying in bed every night and making imaginary love to all the sophomore girls in our school, and a good many of the juniors.

Years afterward I sometimes thought of reminding my mother of her fish lecture. Maybe we could laugh about it, at last. I might make a joke and tell her that when I got married and wanted to become a father, I jumped in the creek and swam around looking for underwater nests to fertilize. But I decided she would never see the humor in it, and let the matter die.

In 1936 I returned to Fort Worth on a schoolbus to attend the Texas Centennial Celebration. This event marked the anniversary of our independence from Mexico, won in the Texas Revolution fought a hundred years before.

During this celebration, which went on almost the entire year, our state earned a reputation as a place where little children were taught to worship their own history, their state's history, that is, instead of their nation's. This was looked on by outsiders as self-centered and provincial.

I can't recall any Texas parent or teacher accusing young Texans of having too much interest in state history, though. In fact, I can't recall from 1936 even one individual among my contemporaries who had an exceptional interest in history of any kind, state, local, national, world, ancient, or modern.

I mustn't speak for the girls but the boys in my bunch were interested in attending the Centennial in Fort Worth for a reason that had nothing whatever to do with history. They wanted to go because the celebration was rumored to be one big sex show. Billy Rose, the theatrical producer, got up an extravaganza in a huge night club called Casa Mañana and its foremost attraction was Sally Rand dancing naked. No revolution, not even the American one in 1776, could compete for our interest with a naked dancer. Another drawing card on the Centennial grounds was a place called Sally Rand's Nude Ranch which had a show featuring buxom girls with bare breasts. History? What history were they talking about?

Sally Rand's dancing was a disappointment to me and the friends I was sitting with. Our seats were a good city block from the stage and Miss Rand looked like a midget from that far. Furthermore, all the time she danced she stayed mainly behind this big bubble and we had arguments on whether she was naked or not. Some said she was wearing a kind of long underwear, real thin and tight-fitting. I voted that she had nothing whatever on. Seemed to me you got more for your money voting that way.

The Nude Ranch was even a greater disappointment because none of our delegation could get in. We weren't old enough. But that didn't keep us from telling fibs about the place when we got back to school. Lots of the guys said they lied about their age and went right on in. Even when you knew a boy wasn't telling the truth, you paid attention to him when he talked in the restroom about being close enough to a bare-breasted girl to reach out and touch her.

"Hey, listen, I'm tellin' you, she wasn't two feet away from me and she was nekkid as a baby rat from her belt buckle up."

The Texas Centennial Celebration did not lead me into the interest I now have in the state's history. If you had asked me the day I got out of high school what significant event took place in Texas in 1936, I would have said '36 was the year Sally Rand danced naked in Fort Worth.

The Nickels

I HAVEN'T MENTIONED it now for a chapter or two but that doesn't mean my family had stopped moving. From the apartment house on Commerce we moved up on Oak Street into the best house we ever lived in. It was called an airplane bungalow because it had one upstairs room that sprouted in an unexpected way out of the main roof. That room became mine, the first I had ever had all to myself. I loved this house.

Our circumstances kept gradually improving. There was a garden spot behind the house and a double garage and a lot where the cow could be kept. We had got that nice Willys-Knight with the bad clutch and we bought an electric icebox, a refrigerator, our first one.

The payment on that refrigerator was five dollars a month. When the men brought it and plugged it in, all of us crowded around while they gave us a lesson on how to fill the ice trays and put them in the freezer compartment. After the men left we sat by the refrigerator and waited for ice. Now and then I would open the door and jiggle a tray to check and my mother would say, "If you don't stop opening the door the water will never freeze." Which was true enough but two or three minutes later, she would be the one opening the door to check the trays. When the water froze, she made tea in the middle of the afternoon so we could have iced tea with our own ice.

Not counting the car, that refrigerator was the first major possession we acquired after all our things went poof in the warehouse. It became a symbol of our rise out of poverty, our return to respectability.

You understand that when we rented a house it needed to be furnished because we had nothing to put in it. There was one advantage to this. In a furnished house we sometimes got the use of a luxury we'd never have had any other way.

For example, that airplane bungalow had a radio in the living room. A big console model. We'd never owned a radio. We had listened to the radios of neighbors but never one of our own. Ima Ruthie tells how she used to sit out in the side yard when we lived on Bewick Street in Fort Worth and listen to Amos and Andy on Mrs. Horn's radio. Mrs. Horn was our next-door neighbor. When she saw Ima Ruthie sitting out there she would turn up the volume. Ima Ruthie also heard on that radio all the songs that were then popular. She could play and sing them immediately but she did have to hear them first.

So the big radio in the bungalow was another miracle, even greater than the electric icebox. It brought all the music of the world into our house. It changed our lives. It made us new and special friends. Ma Perkins. Stella Dallas. Fibber Magee and Molly. Fred Allen and Jack Benny. Little Orphan Annie. Amos and Andy. The Green Hornet. All those Barbours, the members of One Man's Family. And then The Shadow. Who knows what evil lurks in the minds of men? The SHADOW knows.

We got a telephone, too. Our number was 567J. Most everybody on our block on Oak Street had a telephone but on the dirt streets behind us were neighbors who had no phones or electric iceboxes or even indoor toilets. They would come to our house and use the phone. This was not a bother to us. We felt privileged to provide the service. I can see my mother instructing neighbors on how to use the phone. Some would try to talk into the receiver instead of the mouthpiece. Some would think, if they talked to a person way on the other side of town, that they needed to shout in order to be heard.

So in one sense we began to feel a little sophisticated, knowing how to do things that others did not. Yet we clung to many of our country habits. I almost burned that airplane bungalow to the ground, for instance, with a hot brick.

The first winter we lived there was exceptionally cold and we always slept with hot bricks at our feet. One way we could tell when bedtime was near in winter was that our mother would put the bricks on the stove to get hot. They would then be wrapped in old blankets and newspapers and shoved down in the covers so you could stick your feet to a hot brick. It was a very good feeling to poke your toes down in a frigid bed and find that warmth.

If the brick was heated just right and properly wrapped, it would stay warm all night. In many households at breakfast you would hear the question, "Did you sleep well?" At our house in winter the question was, "Did your brick stay warm?" If the answer was yes, it meant you had slept well and didn't get cold feet.

One night I came awake about 2 A.M. and my room was full of smoke. I thought, Well, the house is on fire again and this time I will make a better job of being a hero. But the fire turned out to be my hot brick. It had burned through its wrapping and had set my blankets to smoldering. I gathered up the smoking thing and went downstairs and put it in the bathtub and turned on the water, and this was the nearest I ever came to being a real hero in a house fire.

One good and encouraging thing happened in that house and I got to see it. My father was home. That alone was enough to put me in a good humor because it meant I didn't have to get up at 5:30 and milk. He had come home from a good trip. When he went off on his travels and had sold a lot, he would always tell us about it. When he said nothing about his trip, we knew he had not done well.

This time he had apparently done the best in a long time.

The night before, at supper, he had told some little jokes he had heard on the road. Then we had all gathered around the big radio and listened to the Grand Ole Opry out of Nashville and it was a fine homecoming.

When I came into the kitchen the next morning he was stomping on the back porch. He had gone back to making his loud noises, banging buckets and slamming doors. He had just finished milking so it was around 6:30 A.M. My mother was cooking her everlasting oatmeal. My father brought the milk bucket in, set it on the cook table, and grabbed my mother and began dancing her around on the kitchen floor and singing an old song.

"Buffalo gal woncha come out tonight, and dance by the light of the moon."

He was feeling so fine he had to dance that way, and sing, early in the morning. It had been years since I saw anything as encouraging as that. My mother tried to frown, to pretend she didn't like those early-morning high jinks in the kitchen. But she couldn't frown. She liked it.

From the airplane bungalow we moved down on Daugherty Street to what we called Miss Bell's house. It was almost a hotel, the biggest house we'd ever lived in. We turned it into a boarding house, and my mother rented out rooms and fed boarders for about a year. She worked herself almost sick in that place. I didn't have a lot of loafing time myself. I began milking two cows instead of one and I set up a milk route, not to make money for myself but to pay the bill at the feed store.

Miss Bell was a retired schoolteacher and this old house was her former home. It was a country-style place, right near the middle of town. It resembled a giant boxcar, two stories tall, with about a dozen bedrooms. It had outbuildings. Barns. Cowsheds. A big garden plot.

At the very time my cow-milking chores increased, I began to resent them. I was getting pretty tall and wanted to come out for basketball but I couldn't because basketball practice ran way late in the afternoon, past the time I had to milk and do my route.

I heard students talking about how late they slept and I was amazed. All they did was get up, dress, eat breakfast, and come to school. I decided I was getting a raw deal. When my father was gone, which was almost all the time, I got up before dawn, milked the cows, strained the milk, poured it up into jars, then took both cows out and staked them on vacant lots to graze, and cleaned up and went to school.

I thought eating lunch in the school cafeteria would be a great privilege. I don't believe I ever did it. At noon I trotted home and got the cows and led them to water, then took them back out again and staked them in a fresh place. I'd eat lunch and trot back to school.

I felt married to those cows. After school I had more cow duty. Bring them in, water them, feed them, and milk. Pour up the milk and do my deliveries. Seven days a week.

I delivered on foot unless my father was home with the car. When he was, he talked about getting me some transportation for delivering milk. Today that term, transportation, would mean some kind of car or truck. To my father it meant a bicycle. I didn't expect to get even a bicycle. By the time I did, I was nearing the end of my junior year in high school and many of my friends were already driving their parents' cars around town. I would go peddling along a street with my milk and here would come a friend of mine in a car with a girl sitting close beside him and she would always be the very girl I happened to be in love with. I blamed all this on cows. Without those cows I would be playing basketball and maybe sinking a forty-foot basket at the final buzzer and beating Ranger and being a hero. How was a guy ever going to be a hero delivering milk?

One of my customers was a family way across town from us. I delivered a quart of milk to that house every day for two years without collecting any money. This was because we were obligated to them. I'm not sure what the obligation was but it must have been deep. I believe it had to do with a favor those people had done us when we were down and out. Anyhow, my mother was discharging that obligation with milk.

I remember the final quart. I was leaving to make the route and she held up the jar meant for that family and she looked at it closely to be sure it was sealed right. For a second I thought she was going to shake it. She didn't shake it but she said firmly, "This is the last one." I don't believe she had the numbers down on paper but I know they were in her head and that she knew exactly when we had repaid the debt, with a ten-cent quart of milk per day for two years. She was, as I have mentioned, a woman who kept accounts.

From the boarding house we moved over on Mulberry Street.

It didn't bother me that we moved so much. I had gotten used to it. One day I would come home and they would say, "We're moving Saturday." And we'd just pack up and move. It wasn't any big deal.

My mother had a ritual for the first evening meal served in the new place. She would get out this big iron skillet and scramble a lot of eggs and make toast. I came to associate scrambled eggs with moving. That skillet would always be packed in a handy place so it could be easily found. It didn't matter to me whether the kitchen in the new house was bigger or smaller, better or worse, than the one we had left. As soon as I saw my mother breaking eggs and heating up that big skillet, the new place was home.

I wish I had a piece of toast, right now, made the way she made it. It was toasted in the oven and just a little bit burned. That's the way we liked it. The slice of bread would be almost black around the edges. Its color would fade into a golden brown toward the center. Then there were four round spots of melted butter, positioned on the toast as precisely as spots on dice. Black, brown, and yellow toast. I have tried many times to make toast like that but I can never get it to come out of the oven looking the way my mother's toast looked at supper on moving day.

Every time we moved I would have to keep returning to the old house to get Jiggs. He didn't like to move and he might stay several days at the house we had left.

His favorite place was the airplane bungalow, because it was near the school. He enjoyed young people and hung around the school a lot. Professor Collum, the band director, would let Jiggs into the band room on cold days and he would sleep beneath the director's desk while horn lessons were being given and the band practice was going on. "Old dog's got an ear for music," Professor Collum said.

I almost never got Jiggs to move from the bungalow to the boarding house. Then, about the time he was willing to call the boarding house home, we moved again. He was puzzled and disgusted about it.

It was important for Jiggs to know where we happened to be living because he had a lot of places to go and things to do and some of his expeditions would last several days. When he got ready to return he needed to know where we were because he might need help. Those trips were hard on him.

This old dog knew his purpose: To populate the world with curly-coated black-and-brown puppies. He discharged this responsibility with a mighty zeal. When summoned he would go and do his duty. I have seen him when he received the call. He'd be sleeping in the grass and suddenly his head would lift and his nose would bob, reading the wind. There it was, the message.

He would rise and shake himself and look at me and say, "I've been called." Off he'd trot, following his nose, traveling absolutely along a straight line. Nothing could keep him from going.

Sometimes he would return in a pitiful shape, all chewed up and bleeding. He had to compete with a gang of younger males and there would be dreadful fights. His fangs were smooth when he came to live with us. No telling how old he was those last two or three years he answered the call.

One morning Mr. Gibson, a farmer who lived out by East-land Lake, found Old Jiggs in a ditch on a country road and brought him back to town. I can see that man lifting my dog out of the bed of his little truck, holding Old Jiggs so gently, like a person carrying a baby. Mr. Gibson said, "He may not make it, this time."

No veterinarian practiced in our town. People doctored their own animals. For a week I thought Old Jiggs wouldn't last through the night. He was so weak. His mouth was ripped up and he couldn't eat. My mother fixed him warm soft food, like mush or oatmeal, with pure cream in it and a raw egg or two. We would hold his mouth open and spoon it down.

He would lie on his side and moan, weak and haunting, the sound coming from deep inside where he hurt so bad. "O-O-O-O-O-O-O-O-O-o-o-o-o-o-o-o-o . . ." Ima Ruthie and I sat and stroked him and cried with him.

But one day he struggled to his feet, wobbled to his water pan, and drank.

Not a month later I was doing the evening milking. Old Jiggs always came up close to the cow lot and lay next to the fence and watched me milk. He was not yet well. He was still limping, and his mouth hadn't healed. I happened to be watching him when the musk came to him again on the breeze. He lifted his muzzle to it but he didn't get up directly. I didn't think he would go. When he finally got to his feet he did it slowly, and didn't shake himself because he was still sore.

He went to the corner of the house and stopped and I tried to talk to him. Don't go. Not this time. You're not ready yet. You can't survive another campaign right now, with all that fighting.

He went on anyhow. I suppose he had no choice. When he limped away, along that straight line, I felt I would not see him again.

But within a week he was back. Not without damage but not as severe as the previous campaign. He fell into his box and stayed there three days. A tough old dog. He survived two more years after that close shave and made several more trips. One night over on Mulberry Street he went to bed and didn't wake up. That day you could have irrigated a garden with our tears.

About forty-five years after that weepy day, I was back in Eastland, poking around, stirring up memories to use in this book. I walked to the cemetery to visit the graves of my parents, and I saw Old Jiggs. Here he was alive again, in one of his descendants. I called his name and he stopped and looked at me. He saw nothing to interest him and trotted on. I told my sisters I'd seen Old Jiggs, ten or fifteen times descended from himself, trotting across the cemetery. They grinned. But I could not mistake the distinctive black-and-brown color pattern, or the row of curly hair along the back. I also recognized that resolute trot, the way his nose pulled him along in a straight line toward a place where work needed doing.

My junior year in high school, my mother began talking to me about getting a job so I could save money for college. She said my sisters could get along without a college education but in those modern times, a boy needed a degree. I wasn't much impressed by those talks. I had no idea what I would study if I went to college.

Some of my friends were talking about college but they all knew what they wanted to do with their lives. They wanted to be coaches or lawyers or ranchers or professional athletes. All I knew was, I didn't want my life to have anything to do with cows, and I was still obsessed with the notion of being some kind of hero.

My bicycle got me a part-time job at Western Union, delivering telegrams. Some of the duties I didn't like, such as delivering death messages. "Dad died Sat funeral 2 Pm Mon Albany Baptist Church." I had to wear a Western Union cap and people associated that with bad news. I learned the look of fear on faces. The tight eyes and set mouth. I learned how a face could expand and almost explode with relief and happiness when a telegram turned out to be good news instead of bad.

But the worst of that job was pumping around town on a bicycle and being passed by girls my own age, driving cars.

My second or third day on the Western Union job I delivered a wire way out on Daugherty Street to the Lewis residence. I handed Mr. Lewis the yellow envelope and started walking away and he said, "Wait a minute." He dug in his pocket and handed me a dime. I didn't know what it was for. I told him there was no charge for the telegram, that it had been paid for by the person who sent it to him. I know he was grateful to get that information.

"It's for you," he said. "It's a tip."

I swear to heaven I didn't know what a tip was. Mr. Lewis stood there in his front door and explained it to me. I had never heard anything stranger, the idea of a person giving out money he didn't really have to give. All the time I rode that bike for Western Union, I never got another tip, and didn't expect one.

Between my junior and senior years I took a part-time job at the municipal swimming pool, mainly helping to clean the pool. This paid no money but it got me a free ticket to go swimming any time I wanted to. Which was a considerable payment, in my view, because the pool was the best place in the universe to have imaginary sex with girls. You didn't even have to undress them because they were already in skimpy little bathing suits.

For most of the summer I worked on becoming a champion diver. Girls admired divers. The guy who won the diving contest on the Fourth of July was a very big man indeed. The city sponsored a bathing beauty contest, and a diving competition, and a great fireworks show that night. Everybody attended.

I stood motionless on the high board, waiting for just the right moment to make my final dive. I looked out over a sea of faces, all turned directly toward me. People had heard of me from great distances, possibly as far away as Breckenridge. They had come to see me do my two-and-a-half somersault in the pike position, off the high board. Few divers, even in Abilene sixty miles west, would attempt this dive, and none at all in our part of the country, except me. I made my approach. I knew when I left the board that the dive would be excellent. When I surfaced, the crowd was on its feet, cheering. Every judge gave me a perfect score and I was awarded the championship. That night during the fireworks show I sat in a place of honor next to the girl who won the beauty contest. The runner-up sat on my other side. We were still in our swimsuits and both those beautiful girls scooted up close to me and I could feel the cool smoothness of their thighs against mine.

I never did learn to do any kind of fancy dive but I loved the swimming pool. This was where I first observed the curious custom of burning the skin, so that it would be brown instead of white. In the country we had always covered as much of ourselves up as possible so the sun wouldn't burn us. But suddenly all the young people in our town wanted to be burned brown.

Swimming parties became popular. We played childish games in mixed groups. Games such as tag, which we hadn't played since we were six. But now it was interesting again because it was a way for us to touch one another. Playing tag in the pool, you could even touch a girl's bare thigh by accident. I could think of no other way to touch a girl's bare thigh. Later on I discovered it was possible to do it on purpose but I didn't know it during the tag games.

Taking jobs that paid no cash salary was not doing much to help me save money for college. So I went to work at Tombs and Richardson Drugstore, as a soda skeet. The pay was seventeen and a half cents an hour. On a Monday, say, I would go to work at 8 A.M. and put in eight hours. But on Tuesday, and all alternate days, I opened the store at 7 A.M. and worked until it closed at 11 P.M. I got an hour off for supper and I'd go home and milk the cows. On those long days I made more than $2.50, which was counted pretty fair pay for a high school person.

Skeeting soda was a good job for a guy because the drugstores were social centers. Girls would park out front and get curb service and sit there for hours and enjoy being seen. You may think I was paid a low salary but let me tell you why a soda fountain could not support a large payroll:

I'm behind the fountain. Two girls drive up, park, and honk. I go out and take their order. One wants a cherry Coke and one wants a fountain Dr. Pepper. I go back in, make the drinks, put them on a tray, carry them out and hook the tray on the car window. Maybe an hour later they honk me back out to get the tray and collect for the drinks. Their bill—ten cents. One of them gives me a quarter. I go back in with the tray, take a dime out of the quarter and run back out with fifteen cents change and thank them ever so much for the business. I have made four trips out to that car and grossed ten cents for the store, and this was a common transaction.

Many businesses were running mighty close to the wind. In that drugstore we offered a super-duper banana split for twenty cents. But we kept no bananas. Because they would probably go black before anybody came in and ordered a split. When anybody did order one, I would roll up my apron, tuck it into my belt, dash across the courthouse square to Piggly Wiggly Grocery and buy one banana and sprint back and make a split.

I did that many times. One day I had gone after a banana and set the split out before the customer and he had acquired a companion since he put in the order. Companion said, "Hey, that looks scrumptious. Bring *me* one of those." I drew a heavy breath and took off again to Piggly Wiggly. I didn't see anything very wonderful about that until years afterward.

These were busy times. Our town was waking up, coming

out of the Depression sleep. We observed something called First Monday, which gave us one big county-wide celebration per month. Our merchants sponsored entertainment events to attract people to town. We had rodeos, prize fights, medicine shows. The Human Fly came and walked a tightrope strung across a downtown street. He climbed the south face of the courthouse, while hundreds of us stood on the sidewalks and gasped and oh'd and ah'd.

At Thanksgiving it was decided that turkeys would be given away, but in an extraordinary manner. They would be flung, one at a time, off the roof of the courthouse, six stories high. Turkeys were then leaner and stronger of wing. They spent their lives ranging free, chasing grasshoppers and flying across creeks. From the roof of the courthouse such a bird could flap and soar a great distance. Over Carl Johnson's Dry Goods. Over the Majestic Theater. The Engleman Hotel. The rodeo grounds. Over Pipkin's Warehouse and the T&P Depot and into the thicket where the hobo jungle was, on the north side of the railroad. Those who caught a turkey could keep it, and this was good training for members of the football team, who caught them all.

That was the only year turkeys were thrown off the courthouse. An organization called the Society for Prevention of Cruelty to Animals put up an objection. We had heard of that group but didn't imagine it would ever pay any attention to anything that went on in our town. We were beginning to join the world.

I began to enjoy church for the first time. The Methodists had something called League which met about five o'clock Sunday afternoons. It was a religious organization but it also served as a kind of informal dating bureau. After the meeting you could get a girl to go to the drugstore and sit there and wait for dark, and on the way back to church you might get to do a little smooching in the shadows of the cedar trees.

The Methodists also had a Sunday School teacher, Mrs. Crowell, who spoke a sentence that improved my life. She said she didn't believe in hell. At least she didn't believe in the fire. She didn't believe that sinners when they died would be pitched onto a bed of coals to sizzle forever.

That certainly got my attention. This was not some dude just wagging his tongue on a street corner. This was Mrs. Crowell, Methodist mother and Sunday School teacher, saying she didn't believe in hellfire. Her words were poetry to me.

My life had become close to perfect, with two exceptions. One was those cows, which I longed to get rid of. The other was the lingering fear of eternal damnation and tortuous punishment when I died. Mrs. Crowell gave me hope, on hell. If she was right, maybe hell wouldn't be so dreadful. I didn't see how I would quite avoid going there because the rules of our religion were just impossible.

The toughest one was that even if you *thought* about committing a sin, it was just as bad as if you had actually committed it. No way I could handle that. I could refrain from actual sinning but to refrain from thinking about it was out of the question. By the time I was fifteen I had thought enough sins to send an angel twisting into hell.

To illustrate: At one place we lived (never mind which) we had a neighbor girl who was most outstanding in the figure department. She was bad about sunbathing, too. That girl ruled my life without knowing it. Every time she appeared to me I would leap on her and ravish her. I ravished her everywhere. The back yard. The front porch. In the garage. Any place I could catch her. I didn't count, but in the year we lived near her, I ravished her at least twice a day. I scarcely had time to do anything else. When I did, I went out and ravished other girls.

Now, at church we were admonished to keep our minds and hearts and bodies free of sin because we never knew when we'd be called. When we'd *die,* is what that meant. Death could come like a thief in the night, so be prepared.

I imagined that I would be delivering milk and a truck would hit and kill me. On the Day of Judgment I would stand before the presiding angel, or whoever was in charge, and he would say, "Have you sinned?"

"Yes sir." You had to tell the truth because he already knew the answer to the question and was just checking you for honesty.

"What sin have you committed?" he'd ask.

"Girl-ravishing," I'd say.

"Ah ha. And how many did you ravish?"

"Dozens. Hundreds. All I could."

"Did you ravish them in fact, or in your mind?"

"Only in my mind."

"Well, you know the rule. Thinking about it is the same as actually doing it." He would turn to the doorkeepers then and say, "Fling him in the pit."

But, if Mrs. Crowell was right, and no such thing as a fiery pit existed, maybe I could stand up to hell after all. Maybe the Devil would just put me to breaking rocks with a sledgehammer, or digging postholes, or milking his cows. I decided to believe Mrs. Crowell was right, and I believe it to this time.

Softball came to our town, and our volunteer firemen built a lighted field down by the railroad track. Almost every boy and young man who could trot to first base joined a team and we played under the lights in summer. I got on a team sponsored by the Coca-Cola plant.

The town sponsored a girls' team that played girls from other places. Ima Ruthie was an outfielder on that team, and a heavy hitter. Our girls went to Fort Worth to a state tournament and Ima Ruthie was chosen on the all-state team and received a trophy.

That was the sort of thing I needed to do, win a trophy, preferably much bigger than Ima Ruthie's. I could always catch a ball, if I could get to it, but I couldn't hit my weight. I decided therefore to be practical and become a hero at catching a ball instead of hitting one.

This was a game that decided the championship of a tournament being played at Firemen's Park. I was in left field. It was the bottom of the last inning. If we could get the side out, we would win the tournament. Two were away but the bases were loaded and the opposition had its big slugger at bat. The count was full. Here came the pitch. The batter swung, and connected. A long, high drive. I could see it would go over my head and into the weeds along the T&P tracks. But I did a wonderful thing. The steel light pole in left field had a metal spike sticking out of it about nine feet from the ground. It was a spike used for climbing the pole. I turned my back on the ball and ran full-out and leaped up and caught the spike with my right hand. I swung up, and out, and reached as high as I could and stabbed the ball one-handed and fell to the ground. The game was over and we had won. They awarded us a trophy and my teammates voted to give it to me, personally. It was twice as big as the one Ima Ruthie got in Fort Worth.

What I did was hit the light pole with my head. The ball bounced into the weeds for a home run and we lost.

I knocked myself coo-coo when I hit the pole. I don't remember anything that happened for several hours afterward. Don't know how I got home. When I came to, as we said then, I was sitting on the bed taking my pants off. My folks hustled me down to the hospital. I remember my mother telling the doctor, "He's not supposed to get hit in the head."

I had lost count of the severe blows to the noggin I had collected since that doctor in Fort Worth had told me not to get any. The collision with the light pole did the same as all the others. It raised a knot on my skull that's still there.

In our town there was one disgrace that a young fellow was obliged to avoid, at any cost. He was not supposed to be a virgin when he graduated from high school. If he got deep into his senior year and still hadn't gotten any sex, he grew anxious and began trying harder. If graduation approached and he still hadn't gotten it, he lied and said he had.

The guys who claimed to be sexually experienced and carried condoms in their billfolds would give lectures in the restroom, just as Edgar had done for us back in George Clarke Elementary. The word was, "You got to leave town to get it. Home girls won't put out because they're afraid you'll talk and their folks will hear about it. It's always easier for out-of-town guys. Go to Ranger or Cisco and you'll have better luck. It's the same for those old boys over there. Ranger and Cisco guys can't get it at home but they can come over here and get it from Eastland girls."

I saw the logic in that. I began to look for ways to get to Ranger. I was running late, it seemed to me. This was the fall of '38 and I would graduate the next spring. My problem was transportation. I still didn't have a driver's license. Not that a license mattered much, since no car was at home for me to drive. I began wondering if there was a record of a guy ever peddling a bicycle ten miles to Ranger and finding a girl to relieve him of his virginity.

The popular phrase then was "put out." We spoke of whether certain girls would put out, or wouldn't. My understanding from the restroom lectures was that practically every girl in Cisco would. I finally arranged to ride to Cisco with a fellow who dated a girl there every Friday night. His friend got me a date. He told me, "Be prepared, now. These are Cisco girls, you know what I mean?" Getting ready to go that night, putting on my talcum powder and Brilliantine, I was nervous as a bridegroom. So it was going to happen, at last. A Cisco girl. Would she hop in the back seat and start peeling off her clothes and grabbing at my belt buckle?

She was a preacher's daughter. The entire evening she talked about next year, when she was going away to attend Abilene Christian College.

Later that year I managed a ride to Ranger, too, where I got more conversation. I was discouraged. I supposed I needed to start lying, or I'd be disgraced. But I hated to do it. You could always tell when a guy was lying about girls. He was too casual, and simply not convincing.

"How'd you do in Ranger Friday night?"

"All the good, man. Did all the good."

"You mean she put out?"

"Damn right she put out."

The next week this same guy would have been to Cisco, where he also did all the good. Then he'd go and do it all in Gorman, or Rising Star, or Desdemona, or Morton Valley. He'd try to have you thinking he had girls putting out for him in three counties, and you knew it wasn't so. I didn't mind telling a fib but I didn't want to *sound* like I was fibbing.

I will make a small boast here, about the sort of reverse-English system I developed to deal with this serious problem. I simply didn't lie. When anybody asked me about sex, I told the truth, and nobody believed me. They couldn't accept that a guy would keep on dating girls and admitting he didn't *get* any.

They would ask, "How'd you do out at the lake last night? You get any?"

I would say no, which was true.

"Aw, come on," they'd say. "You ashamed of it or something?"

I would say no, I wasn't ashamed of it but I just didn't get any. They figured I was being foxy, that I had really done all the good but didn't want to share the details. That's what they wanted, a description of how it went. Pretty soon I didn't have a friend left who would believe anything I said about sex, and every word I spoke about it was true. I was proud of my system. I got a reputation as a guy who was very active in the field of sex but who just wouldn't admit it. That's how I avoided disgrace.

The night I walked down the aisle to graduate, I was eighteen and I'd had the same amount of sex as that preacher's daughter in Cisco, which was none at all.

In this history I have been hesitant to mention very many of my classmates and friends by name. The reason is, they get nervous when I start putting their names in print and I don't want to cause them discomfort.

But I can't do without a mention of Dude. Dude Wilkins. We were close friends all through high school. We liked to do the same things. Except dance. Dude wasn't high on dancing. He didn't fall in love with every skirt that flounced by, either. But he had an older brother who had taught him about hunting and fishing and cars and electricity and Dude tried to teach me the same things and we had a good time at it. We seldom disagreed. We loved the woods and wild things. We roamed.

We were about fourteen, when we began. In summer when my father came home and stayed a few days and I didn't have to milk, I would sleep at Dude's house out on the west edge of town. We would get up at some ridiculous hour, like 3:30 A.M., and carry long cane poles out to Eastland Lake and we'd be fishing for channel cat long before dawn. When the sun set we'd be out there still, not wanting to quit, complaining about the shortness of days.

Sometimes we didn't hunt or fish at all but simply wandered, over miles and miles of scrub timber and rocky prairie. We'd find a little stream that seemed fed by a spring, and trace it up through heavy thickets to its source, and drink there. We'd go to cliffs on the Leon River miles from town and roll boulders off the rims and enjoy the great splashes they made. We'd find old houses, abandoned long ago, and chunk the windows out of them and nobody cared. We'd dig for buried treasure that wasn't there. From junk heaps we'd gather rusty parts to build a car we never built.

We clung so hard to boyhood.

When we were seventeen and eighteen we struggled together through that strange time of being half boy and half man. One minute we'd think of making love to girls and the next we'd go back to being fourteen again, and find comfort in doing a thing that youngsters do. Like pitching bottles in the river, with stoppers in them. Watching them float around a bend and disappear. Thinking of where they'd go. All the way down the Leon River and into the Brazos and into the

Gulf of Mexico and then—maybe half around the world to Africa, or Australia, where they'd wash up on a beach and be picked up by—hey, by beautiful naked native girls.

When we sensed our time together was growing short, we became sentimental and emotional and embarrassed by our feelings. One weekend we went with Dude's father to fish on Deep Creek in Callahan County. We weren't catching much so we roamed, and came to a certain ledge where we'd been before. It overlooked a pretty swale, with pecan trees and fresh green grass. This was a good place and we stayed there a long while and looked down.

Without talking about it very much, we left something on that ledge. Dude had two buffalo nickels in his pocket and we scooted them back into a crack in the ledge. We marked the place by two young mesquites.

"One of these times," Dude said, "we'll come back here and find them."

I wondered, years later, whether he understood exactly what the two coins represented. I didn't, not at the time. But very soon it would become clear enough to me what it was we left there on the ledge.

The summer of '39, my folks astonished me by announcing that they were going to sell the cows and move to Lubbock.

I didn't care anything about moving to Lubbock but I was certainly in favor of selling the cows. The last year I milked those creatures, right there in the middle of town, they became an almost unbearable social albatross.

A cattle buyer stopped at our house and talked to my father about two minutes and bought those old Jerseys. He said he would give us a dollar extra if I'd lead them out and turn them loose in Lyerla's pasture. The buyer gave my father the cash and I snapped the chains onto the cows and led them for the last time along the streets of our town. They were going to the country, where cows ought to be. I had been through a lot with those two old sisters but it didn't give me the smallest twinge of regret to unbuckle their halters and shoo them into the mesquite. I stood at the gate and watched them plod into the brush. They didn't even look back.

With one exception that came to pass twenty-three years later, I have since had no direct association with cows.

I had planned a mighty celebration for the day we got rid of the cows but now I was faced with the business of moving to Lubbock. I didn't want to go.

Gradually I had come to love our little town. I liked to go at the end of the day up on the hill, where the city park and the swimming pool are, and sit on a rock. From up there I could see most of the town and I thought it looked just the way a town ought to look. I loved its streets and houses and people and its buildings and trees. I loved its very dirt. At dusk, all the street lights switched on at once and the sight of that filled my chest and made my neck tingle and my eyes wet. Without cows to milk, this would be the best place in all of creation to spend my life.

I had lost the itching foot that Dude and I both had a few years earlier. I changed my mind about floating down the river and seeing the world on a ship, because I didn't want to leave our town. I had given up the idea of going to college, too. You didn't need to go to college to live in Eastland. Men all over that town had homes and pretty good cars and steady jobs and they never had gone to college.

Besides, that savings account I established for college never got off the ground. The work I'd done didn't pay enough to meet my living expenses. Remember that fruit jar full of pennies I saved, from carrying coal oil? "Put them in the bank," my mother had said, "and let them grow to you." But they hadn't grown very much, and I hadn't added to them. They just sat there, for five years in the bank. My junior year I drew them out and bought a secondhand softball glove. I had developed a need for expensive things.

I would have to go to Lubbock with the folks but I swore I would return. I would get myself a job and stay home forever. Ima Ruthie was getting ready to marry a good old boy named Andy Taylor. Andy had gone to Texas A&M and was with the

Agricultural Adjustment Administration. He would help me get a job. Or I might go to work for Pete Cullen, who was dating my sister Maifred and would later marry her. He was maintenance foreman at the power plant out on the Leon River. Dude was going to work for him, and I figured Pete would hire me. I could buy a car, have money to spend on girls, and live in the hotel like Jim Golden. And maybe I would buy my mother a house.

Gloria

L UBBOCK had a population of about 40,000 when we
went there. We were able to increase that figure by
only three because my sisters stayed in Eastland. We never
again all five lived in the same house.

Ima Ruthie moved in with the Coleman family, which already had two or three daughters and seemed not to be bothered by another one. My sister Maifred averted starvation by
quitting her newspaper job. She went to work for a lawyer
and made a huge salary, something like $120 a month. I think
that's close to the correct figure. She made enough, at any
rate, to move into the Connellee Hotel where nobody lived
unless they were knocking down a lot of money.

In September of '39, something unexpected happened to
me. I became a college student.

One of the reasons my folks moved to Lubbock was that it
had a state-supported college, Texas Tech. Tuition there was
twenty-five dollars per semester. After you paid that, and
your student fees, and bought your books, you spent about
fifty dollars to attend this institution for a term. I don't know
where the handsome sum of fifty dollars came from but I suspect from my sister Maifred back in Eastland.

I thought the campus of Texas Tech, among the places I
knew that claimed to be civilized, was the most desolate.
Parts of its grounds were the same as the front yard in that

house on the Granbury sheep ranch—scoured clean by the everlasting wind. The red tile–roofed Spanish buildings were placed so far apart that when a sandstorm was blowing, a student walking to class could lose his way.

The college had about 4,000 students distributed thinly across a huge campus. Now it's a university with an enrollment of 23,500 and one of the most attractive campuses in the Southwest. I am always surprised to return and find the place beautiful. I didn't think it was possible.

At first I didn't like that school. One reason was, I discovered I was saddled with another social stigma—the fact that I lived with my parents. Nobody could move into the mainstream of college life while living at home. You needed to be free of parental control, so you could stay out all night and drink whiskey and smoke cigarettes and raise hell.

My parents, however, stayed in Lubbock less than a year. One day my father handed my mother and Danny McShane into the front seat of the car and they took off. I moved into a dormitory and for the next two years, my folks didn't live anywhere. They stayed on the road. I know that appealed to my father, as much as it didn't appeal to my mother.

I believe he was saying, "At last, I don't have to go home because there's no home to go to." I believe she was saying, "There's no home, but at least he has taken me with him."

Danny McShane was a dog, a nervous, eccentric fox terrier. Before we left Eastland my father had made one of his dramatic entries, bearing a gift. It was a puppy in a shoe box. It was named for a professional wrestler my father admired. The pup was supposed to be for me, to replace Old Jiggs, but I never got him. He was my father's dog from the first.

One reason my mother liked the idea of my attending Texas Tech is that Lubbock County was dry territory. That is, alcoholic beverages could not be legally sold there. She supposed, then, that I would not be tempted to drink any. I never had, at the time I am talking about. The only alcoholic product I had tried was a piece of Christmas fruitcake with a little wine poured over it. It tasted wonderful.

I am thankful now that my mother wasn't aware that Lubbock County was one of the foremost bootlegging centers of the nation. I knew guys living in my dormitory who worked their way through college by bootlegging. They would hitchhike to Amarillo, which had liquor stores, and fill an old suitcase with bad bourbon for about two dollars thirty cents per fifth and hitchhike back to Lubbock and peddle it on the campus for five dollars a bottle.

It was the custom then for freshmen at Tech to be ordered about by upperclassmen, to do whatever an upperclassman said they ought to do. The first assignment I received from a sophomore was to go out and buy a pint of whiskey. Just offcampus there was a drugstore that sold booze by prescription. An old doctor, or at least a fellow posing as one, sat inside the door. You paid him fifteen cents and he scrawled a prescription for a bottle of bourbon or gin or whatever you wanted. A dry town. Ho ho ho.

We had men's social clubs at Tech. These were the forerunners of the Greek fraternities to come later. They had rush parties the same as fraternities. I got invited to one. It was described in advance as a stag picnic, at a lake outside Lubbock.

The member who picked me up was late and we arrived at the site about sundown. I was a little surprised to see that the event was a beer bust. Several kegs were in a line on the lake shore and scores of young men were drinking beer in great earnest out of quart ice-cream cartons. They all appeared to be in various stages of drunkenness.

I had not been around drunks much and I found it very interesting. I could look out over a kind of sweeping landscape and it was decorated liberally with college boys being drunk. Stumbling over rocks and stumps. Shouting obscenities. Urinating. Falling down. I thought of my mother, who wanted me to go to school at Lubbock because it was a dry town.

That night I got my first exposure to this truth: There is nothing as bizarre as a college sophomore full of beer. He has drunk so much his ears seem to be giving off bubbles. He walks the way he has seen drunks walk in movies. Staggering, that is, and his staggers get out of control and he falls but he is not damaged due to his looseness. If somebody tells him he has had too much, he responds by drinking more, and more. His body in this circumstance has more judgment than his mind. When it decides he must quit, it causes him to vomit and he vomits on his shoes. The next morning, when he is finished with his dry heaves, he speaks of what a good time he had the night before. I am trying to think if I know of anything stranger than that.

At that picnic I drank some beer, my first. It was warm, and bitter. It left on my tongue the flavor of a raunchy ice-cream carton.

But on the way home the upperclassman who took me to the lake said a thing of colossal significance: "You ever want any, just sing out."

I asked want any what.

"Pussy, what else? There's plenty around. I can fix you up."

I said I needed fixing up, bad. He said how about tomorrow night? I said yes. Sure. Damn right. You bet. Thank you very much.

Her name was not Gloria. But I have always called her that. I don't know why. She was large. Taller than I was, and overweight. She had a high little voice that didn't fit her. She was kind and had a sweet face. She had huge breasts and thin ankles.

We rode a city bus from College Avenue into downtown Lubbock and went to a movie. I could not tell you what the movie was about. I could not have told you the next day. I could not have told you while we were watching it. She overflowed her seat and seemed almost to surround me. She put her hand on my leg and patted me and all my Stamford packing-crate symptoms came surging forth. The pounding heart. The heat in the face. The tingling and the weakness.

From the theater we walked to Mackenzie State Park, which is not far from downtown. We went to a picnic table. This was her choice. She led and I followed. I did what she said. I would have done anything. Climbed a tree. Jumped in the water.

I do not understand why she did this for me. I have wondered why, so many times.

All I remember is a great warm wet smooth softness. I floated in the softness.

I didn't want him to come into my head but he did: Edgar, grinning in the restroom in Fort Worth, telling how he put it to the girls and made them howl. I didn't make Gloria howl. I made her laugh, though. She said, "You're kind of quick on the trigger, honey."

In addition to that, in Lubbock I got my driver's license.

My folks would come through Lubbock now and then and visit me. I knew they had come when I heard a certain snuffling sound coming under my dormitory door. The sound was made by Danny McShane. My father liked to drive up behind the dorm and put the dog out and let him climb the fire escape and find my room.

My father was an awful fool about that little dog.

They were inseparable and their inseparableness brought about some peculiar scenes. In his travels my father would go into a hotel and he would refuse to inquire beforehand whether it admitted dogs. He had a cardboard box. It contained Danny's blanket and an old black shoe. He would put the dog in there, and hold the box beneath his arm, and walk into a hotel lobby and pick up the pen and start registering. He would place the box on the desk and Danny would sit up in it and watch his master write the words.

Desk clerk would say, "Sir, I'm sorry, the hotel doesn't allow dogs."

My father would not argue or get upset. He would lay down the pen and walk out and try another place.

I was always surprised how many hotels would let him go on in with that terrier, even if they had rules against pets. Sometimes he would be registered and walking to the elevator before the hotel clerk understood what was happening or summoned the nerve to quote him the rule.

That old shoe in the box? If anybody asked him about the shoe my father would say, "That's my dog's shoe." Just as if the dog wore it. What he did with it was exercise. When they got to the room, my father would present Danny with the shoe. The dog would take the loose laces in his teeth and spin round and round, slinging that old shoe. It would bounce off chair legs and glance off thin walls and it was a big shoe, about a size eleven, and bulky, and it made a great racket.

Guests would call the desk and say something loud was going on in 201. The clerk would call 201 and my father would say, "It's just my dog, doing his shoe." He said it in a tone that suggested every guest had a dog that did a shoe.

My folks stayed in the Commercial Hotel when they came to Lubbock. This was a two-story hotel that would accept animals. When I went downtown to visit them I was embarrassed by my father and that dog. They played ball in the lobby. My father would bounce a rubber ball and Danny would leap at it no matter where it bounced. In those times, hotel guests sat round in lobbies a lot because there was no TV or radio in the rooms. I cringed when my father bounced the ball into the newspaper of a guest, and Danny would leap into the person's lap. Very few guests thought this was funny or cute.

It bothered me that my father seemed to be losing something. He was not as smart or clever or handsome as I thought he was when I was a boy. His neck was too skinny and long. He still dressed neatly and I loved him dearly but he didn't know as much as I thought he did. My sophomore year I was taking trigonometry and I mentioned it during one of his visits. He said, "What's trigonometry?"

I was shocked to learn that I knew about a thing that my father didn't know, this man who enlarged my world so much with his travels. It made me sad.

■

I learned to love college life when I moved into Knapp Hall, a new men's dormitory on College Avenue near the main entrance to the school. It was a wonderful place. In the college-boy tradition, we complained about the food in the dining hall but the food was better than any I had ever eaten, at home or anywhere. Room and board in that dorm was twenty-five dollars a month. My sister Maifred sent me that amount, every month. Ima Ruthie helped me, as well.

That war was going on then in Europe and there was talk that one day we might get into the fighting. I didn't think we would, and I had little interest in the conflict or what was causing it. I'd never had things so good, and I didn't want to think of events that might disrupt my life.

The Depression as far as I knew was finished. Even so, goods and services in Lubbock were cheap, cheap, cheap. I could get a pair of slacks cleaned and pressed on College Avenue for nine cents. I could go to a movie for fifteen cents. I got invited to dances and they cost nothing.

A popular social event was the Coke date. If you were low on funds and didn't have enough to take a girl to a movie at fifteen cents a head, you called her in the afternoon for a Coke date. You walked her just across College Avenue to the drugstore and bought her a soft drink for a nickel and danced. The drugstore furnished the music. Total cost of such a date: A dime.

Texas Tech was not known then among institutions of the Southwest for its academic excellence. Even so, it offered far more than I would ever need or could handle. It had a few extraordinary teachers. One was an English professor named Alan Stroud that I got, by the luck of the draw, for freshman composition. He liked my papers. I never got good grades from him because he was impatient with sloppy spelling. But he would let me write about anything. I would do long free-wheeling pieces of fiction about monsters devouring nubile maidens in dark European dungeons. He would say nice things about them, and give me D's for my spelling. He had studied in England. Only the angels of heaven know what he was doing in Lubbock, Texas, but he stayed there his entire professional life and did much good in the world.

Back in Eastland I had had a high school English teacher, Verna Johnson, who had also liked my compositions and encouraged me. The greatest thing she did was to show me that writing words on paper did not have to be torment, as I had previously thought, that the process could be an entertainment and a reward. Therefore sometimes I would write sentences when I didn't even have to be doing it, and this was the gift of Verna Johnson. Then when Dr. Stroud in Lubbock pushed me further along, I began to think maybe writing stories was what I ought to pursue. Still, after I had been in college two years, it had never once struck me that anybody would ever pay me a dime for writing one.

The most important college course I took was Orientation 101. Every student took it as a freshman. There was a joke, "He's so dumb he flunked Orientation." It wasn't possible to flunk Orientation. You met the class once a week and they told you how to get from one building to another to attend class. They told you where to go to the restroom, and what to do if you got sick, and what would happen to you if you didn't behave yourself. The remainder of the time you sat in Orientation and marked squares on aptitude tests, designed to show whether you were suited to study engineering or animal husbandry or home economics or whatever.

At the start of my junior year I was called into the dean's office: Dr. J. M. Gordon, dean of the School of Arts and Sciences. He had my file open on his desk and was frowning. He said:

"You can't just go to college. You've got to declare a major."

I told him I would be glad to major in something but I didn't know what it ought to be. I hadn't any notion what I wanted to study, what I wanted to do with my life.

He frowned again and looked down at my file. He said:

"Judging from your tests back in Orientation, it seems to me that journalism would be a good major for you. Besides, it's an easy major."

I told him fine, good, put me down as a journalism major, and he did.

And so, in that office, in a meeting that didn't last five minutes, the course of my life was determined.

I was told I would need to work on the student newspaper, *The Toreador.* I wasn't much interested in that. I didn't want to be a hotshot reporter who covered murder trials and city halls and police stations and went around asking nosy questions of people who didn't want to answer them. That didn't appeal to me, and it still doesn't.

One day, in order to get a grade, I wrote what was called a feature story. It wasn't a feature story. It was an essay, an opinion piece, a column. It was a silly thing about the telephone system on campus, and how a male student could dial a resident of the women's dormitory for two hours and get nothing but a busy signal. I proposed a solution, which was that the girls and the boys ought to be moved closer together so they could communicate. I stopped far short of saying they ought to be housed in the same dormitory but that was the idea I was working toward.

The editor ran that piece across the bottom of page one, and of course it had to be by-lined. When I saw my name in boldface type below the headline, I was stunned. I was electrified. I had never seen anything so beautiful. I had never liked my first name but, when printed along with the last name that way, it looked splendid. Two, short, punchy, four-letter words. Seeing my name in 12-point Bodoni bold gave me a boot in the seat of the pants that I have never recovered from, and that has been forty-five years ago.

In summer I would go back to Eastland. My folks were still on the road. The first summer I got a job driving a panel truck, delivering clothes for a dry-cleaning shop. A few of my contemporaries were living in the old Maverick Hotel. I got a room there and came close to starving for three months.

A trombone player by the name of Collin Satterwhite grew

up in Eastland. He was a year or two ahead of me. In high school he had led a little dance band. I had learned to play the trumpet, not very well but well enough to read music and keep on the beat, and Satterwhite got me to join his orchestra. This was a wonderful experience. Satterwhite was an excellent musician and a fine trombonist. He ended up playing in Tommy Dorsey's orchestra. All of us bragged about Tex Satterwhite being from Eastland.

When he left his home town, Satterwhite turned the leadership of the band over to Jack Brown, and then E. J. Pryor had it awhile, and the group held together loosely for several years. The summer of '40 when I was driving the tailor shop truck, the band would rent the roof garden of the Connellee Hotel and throw a dance to make money. But not very much. We'd charge a dollar per couple admission and play practically nonstop from eight o'clock until one. The hotel charged us twenty-five dollars for the hall so we didn't do so well. Not many guys then had money to spend on a dance. After we paid expenses we'd divide the take equally and go get a hamburger at the Tip Top Cafe out on the highway. Most times we wouldn't make much more than the price of a hamburger and a Coke, but we didn't care. Making music that way was ever so satisfying. It couldn't have been very good music but we thought it sounded first-rate.

Later on, when I got into the Army and left Texas and discovered other parts of the world and made it known that I liked music, the people I met assumed I liked what we called hillbilly stuff. They supposed that a person from a little West Texas town would never have heard anything but hillbilly, which is what country and Western used to be called.

As far as I know, mighty few young people that I grew up with in Texas were interested in hillbilly. We were trying to break away from that. We loved jazz, and what we called swing music. Which was dance music. Big-band music. The guys in our little orchestra worshipped musicians like Tommy Dorsey, Benny Goodman, Glenn Miller, Les Brown. We didn't play "Turkey in the Straw" or "Home on the Range."

We played "Tuxedo Junction." "Song of India." "String of Pearls." And the sweet snuggle-up ballads like "September in the Rain," and "Mood Indigo."

My personal hero was the great trumpet player Harry James.

We were playing the Aragon Ballroom on the West Coast, my friend Harry and I. I had auditioned for him when he came through Fort Worth and he liked my style. He should have, because it was exactly like his. You could hardly tell the difference between my trumpet and Harry's. Very soon I became his right-hand man. I fronted the band when he was backstage writing love letters to Betty Grable or whatever he did back there. When he came out, sometimes he would motion for me to stay, and stand out front with him, and we would play together for a number. There at the Aragon, when Harry would disappear backstage, people would come up and tell me, "You're every bit as good as he is." I agreed.

At Texas Tech two or three student orchestras played for dances. I tried out for a chair in one of them but I wasn't anywhere near good enough. They said they would call me if they needed me.

The summer of '41 I wanted more money than I thought I could make in Eastland so I went hunting for work. I hitch-hiked up into the Texas Panhandle where, I'd heard, a guy could make money working on ranches. I got a job right away, driving a tractor on the Whitman Ranch south of Amarillo.

I worked up there almost two months and came near dying of loneliness.

A tractor driver stayed in the field from sunup to sunset and he was alone, always, on a great plowed plain. This was the first time I had ever been alone for very long and I was surprised that I didn't like it. I needed somebody to talk to. Never, since that summer, have I spent so many days alone.

Driving that tractor I made a dollar fifty a day plus room and board in a ranch house where nobody talked. There was nowhere to go and nothing to spend my money on so I saved every dollar I was paid. But I couldn't stand the loneliness.

I headed home and stopped in Lubbock on the way. I was in bad need of company and I tried to find Gloria, of the picnic table in Mackenzie Park. But she had gotten married and moved to Dallas.

Two events of considerable significance happened when I was in school for the fall term of '41.

One was that the Japanese decided they wanted to fight a war with us and they flew over and did all that damage to Hawaii.

The other event was that Ima Ruthie broke her Sunday School record. One morning she just didn't feel like going. She was in labor with her first daughter, and stayed home. She had not missed a Sunday in twelve years.

When we got into World War II I figured I would never be accepted into the service and that didn't improve my morale. The best possible way to become a hero was in a war. But what branch of the service would take me, with all my bumps and the bad eye I had from getting hit with the rock that time.

Furthermore, at school they had taken my blood pressure, which had never been taken before. It read 155 over 91, when I was eighteen. Everybody said I was lucky, that I would never have to go to war. That's what we said then about entering the service. Go to war. Even if you didn't get within a thousand miles of a fight, we called it going to war.

I took my draft physical. The young doctor who did the examination told me he didn't know of a rule that disqualified a guy just because he had unexplained knots on his head. He agreed my eye looked abnormal but the vision in it was excellent. Also my blood pressure had come down from the clouds. I passed the physical and was classified 1-A. I felt better.

I began volunteering for things. Most of us did that. We wanted in the war. I decided to become a deck officer in the Navy. I had never seen salt water. I had never been within 300 miles of it but I had read C. S. Forester's Captain Hornblower stories and I saw that a warship was a fine place for heroics.

But the Navy didn't like my eye, despite that it could spot a run in a nylon stocking from 500 feet. I tested for everything the Navy had, including apprentice seaman. But when I went for the physical my blood pressure would celebrate by going up thirty points, or else they wouldn't like my eye and my bumps. Next I tried the Marines. They didn't want me either.

I ran out of places to volunteer. I was one of the most physically examined citizens in Texas. I thought I must be going anemic from blood tests. I decided just to lay back and let the Army draft me, what the hell. I was sick of being poked on and questioned and punctured and bled.

My folks were staying in a hotel in Abilene. I went to see them and got into a conversation with a guy on the street. I don't know who he was. He interested me because he had just passed the physical and the written test to enter the Army Air Corps aviation cadet program.

He said, "You ought to go try it."

I told him I had flunked the most liberal physical exams offered by both the Navy and the Marine Corps and he said, "But the Army's not that tough. You got blood pressure? What you do is take four aspirin just before you go, and you'll pass. Army needs pilots bad."

My common sense combined with my college education told me that couldn't be right but I took both the aspirin and the tests and I passed. I still don't know why. Two days later I was sworn into the Army. They told us they weren't quite ready to start making airplane pilots of us, that we could go on back to work, or school, or whatever we'd been doing, and they'd call us pretty soon.

The reason for this was, the Army was stock-piling potential pilots. It didn't have the facilities then to train them but it wanted them on hold, a sort of pool to draw trainees from.

This was the summer of '42. The war was heating up. I went to San Angelo to work, expecting any day to be called. I didn't get called all summer. The reason for San Angelo, my mother's brother Uncle Roy Oxford came to us and said the Army was building a bombardier training base there and we could make good money. We went for it.

My father quit the road. Traveling men everywhere had quit because tires and gasoline were hard to get. Uncle Roy took a job at the temporary lumberyard on the base and he put me on his payroll at fifty cents an hour, four dollars a day, the most money I'd ever made. My father got work in the payroll department. With Uncle Roy we rented an apartment and all rode to work together.

We sweated out the first payday. We had spent ourselves broke on moving and paying rent in advance. Groceries were getting scarce, and we had a week to go before the money came in from all those new jobs.

Uncle Barney came grinning up. A surprise. Did he mean to go to work at the base with us? Well, no, he didn't think so, not just yet. Thought he'd sort of look around the town first. He didn't spend the night with us.

The next afternoon we had come in from the base and my father and I went out and sat on the front steps, to loaf a little and look at the street. Uncle Barney came slouching up about sundown, making his silent laughter. He pulled something thick out of his pocket. I had to stare at it a couple of seconds before I saw it was a roll of bills, money, U.S. currency. It was the most cash I had ever seen outside a bank. Uncle Barney said, "Found a pretty good little old poker game in town."

We went forth and bought a great load of groceries. Before we got back home Uncle Barney put a couple of coarse-looking bills in my father's hand. No comment passed between them.

This scene strengthened my suspicion that throughout our Hard Times, my father and Uncle Barney looked out for one another when circumstances got desperate, and said nothing about it because gambling was often involved. Uncle Barney came to our house and was fed and housed when he was broke, and I think he paid his debts when he was flush. The Christmas my father showed up at the sheep ranch, bearing all those gifts and we wondered how he bought them? I have to think Uncle Barney had a hand in that.

When the jobs at the bombardier base played out, my father returned to Abilene and took a job as a clerk in a department store. He never went back on the road. The next several years he made a satisfactory living and bought that nice Dodge car. Not a house, though. That would have meant a commitment to stay in one place the rest of his life, and he couldn't handle that. He seemed to scratch his itching foot by moving from house to house instead of town to town. He and my mother stayed in Abilene seven years and I can count seven places they lived, and I may be missing a couple.

When September of '42 came around and I still hadn't been called into the Army I began to get nervous. Most of the guys I knew were already gone. Dude was gone. My buddies who played in the little orchestra in Eastland were gone. Many of my classmates at Lubbock, gone. I was afraid the war would be over and they would all come home with a chestful of medals and there'd I be, left at the post.

I went to Lubbock for my senior year but not with any enthusiasm. I hadn't even reserved a room in the dormitory because I thought by September I'd already be fighting Germans or Japanese. In the dorm office they told me I'd just have to take pot luck on a roommate. That meant that since I hadn't reserved a room and chosen a roommate I wanted to live with, I had to accept the guy who was already in the room. This was considered risky because you might get a bad citizen.

But I had no choice, so I signed up for the room and walked around to the door and opened it and met Bodie McElroy from Waxahachie, Texas, one of the best humans that ever walked in shoe leather.

Five years later he would be the best man at my wedding.

We have not lived near each other since then or kept in especially close touch. But that's not necessary. Right now, if I got arrested and thrown in jail at 2:30 in the morning, I could call old Bo and he would come and get me out. Not a bad fellow to get, taking pot luck.

Bodie makes an interesting study in how much young men wanted in the war then. It will seem strange to those who struggled so hard to stay out of subsequent wars.

When he was in high school Bo was kicked by a horse and the blow shattered his thigh bone. Doctors tried to patch him up by splicing the bone with a metal plate. But the screws pulled loose at one end of the plate and the plate pooched out and the leg was a mess. Doctors told him if they tried to fix it again he would be laid up for months and even then it might not be fixed, so Bo just lived with it. He got around with a limp but he got around fast. He never slowed down. Other than the leg he was healthy and strong. If he'd wanted to he could have picked me up and pitched me out a window.

He was classified 4-F but he refused to accept that he would stay out of the war. He began hounding people. Draft boards. Recruiting officers. Politicians. Bankers and merchants of influence. The fall of '42 it seemed to me he spent the major part of his time writing letters, making phone calls, going to see people, trying to get into the service.

By Christmas, nothing had worked for him. "I haven't given up," he kept saying. But I could tell he was discouraged. Even in those times we had our draft dodgers. I had met a few. What an irony. They were fighting to stay out, and being successful, and there was old Bo fighting to get in, and failing.

I went to Eastland for Christmas that year. I remember a scene that was so cornball and sentimental that I can barely stand to tell you about it. But the scene makes a good demonstration of the emotional state of young people at this time.

We had a Christmas dance at the Connellee Hotel. A lot of the people I had gone through high school with were there. Some of the guys were in uniform, and the rest soon would be. We loved Christmas dances. It seemed to me the girls were always prettier at Christmas, and were feeling generous and sentimental. They would dance a little closer. Stay out a little later.

But this affair didn't work as a Christmas dance. You would see two or three couples just marking time, not really dancing, mainly talking. About ten o'clock the dancing stopped, without any signal, and all of us crowded close on the dance floor and put our arms about one another and began to sing.

We sang old and bittersweet songs from our high school days. The girls all cried, and the boys fought to keep from it. We sang the school song—really, yes—and "America the Beautiful." We bathed in sentimentality.

Some of us made bad little speeches. (I am not going to say whether I did or not.) We spoke of friends, and love, and home, and the goodness of our lives. We spoke lines that would later be unbearable clichés because they would come from the mouths of actors in dozens of bad war films. We said things like, "Soon now, many of us will be going away, because we have a job to do. And some of us won't be coming back."

We actually *said* those things, and they wrenched our spirits, and I am saddened now that they became so cornball. Because they were true. Some of us didn't come back.

I was enrolled at school for my last semester when finally I was called out. When I had packed and was about to go, Bo shook hands with me and said, "I might see you out there somewhere. I still haven't given up."

I went to Dallas and then to Sheppard Field at Wichita Falls for basic training. Before I shipped out of there, I had a letter from Bo. He had gone to Washington to see his Congressman. He had signed a stack of waivers a yard high about his disability, and had got into the Navy.

The War

WHEN THE TROOP TRAIN crossed the Red River and passed into Oklahoma, I was outside Texas for the first time. I went to Wayne, Nebraska, and learned to stand at attention and march in a straight line. From there I went to preflight school at Santa Ana, California, and then to Thunderbird Field in Arizona for primary flight training.

In those travels, I learned that I talked funny. I could walk up to a stranger and ask him what time it was and he would laugh. At Texas Tech I lacked only sixteen semester hours of having a bachelor of arts degree in journalism with an English minor. But nobody had ever told me that I spoke in a Texas accent that would be counted one step from a foreign tongue in places like Chicago or Philadelphia.

One Saturday night in Nebraska I sat in a tavern booth with a pretty girl who was majoring in languages at Wayne State University. She would give me short sentences to say. "Now the town is brown." And, "How high does the goose fly?" As quick as I could get a sentence out, she would start laughing. I had never met anybody so easy to entertain.

At Santa Ana I met a master sergeant who had taught English in a Wisconsin high school. He would ask me to repeat such folksy Texas phrases as "a right nice night." He would grin and take notes. He showed me how I pronounced those words. "Uh rot nahs not."

I began to get self-conscious about my speech. I had never been the best talker, even at home. Now everybody wanted me to talk faster. I would go into the post exchange at Santa Ana and begin a sentence that was going to end up ordering a chocolate malt but about halfway through it the Brooklyn guy behind the counter would say, "OhforcrysakebuddyIaintgotallnightcomeonspititout." I didn't understand that. I didn't even know what language he was speaking. A college education out of Lubbock had not prepared me for these problems.

The first time I got in an airplane I was supposed to fly it. But when they showed me how the controls worked, I knew I would never learn to operate them, and I didn't. The trouble could be traced back to the homemade carts we built when I was a kid in Eastland. We built them for two or three summers and rolled them down Ammerman Street from the high school all the way to Commerce. The carts were distant kin to the Soap Box Derby carts we saw in the newsreels at the picture show.

One of those carts was the simplest of all vehicles, consisting of a thick plank attached to two sets of wheels. The front axle pivoted on a sort of spindle bolt. You sat on the board and steered with your feet, by pressing right or left on the front axle.

If you wanted to turn left, you pushed with your right foot. This made the right wheel move ahead of the left wheel and the result was a left turn. Do you see how it worked? It was a perfectly reasonable system of steering to me, and I had proved to myself that it worked by rolling down Ammerman Street forty dozen times. I had even saved my personal neck by jamming my left foot against the axle when I needed a desperate right turn to miss a substantial obstacle. Such as a telephone pole or a fire plug.

Before I looked inside an airplane, I supposed that the rudders would work that same way. They do not.

When I was growing up I had no special interest in airplanes. I wanted ships, but the Navy wouldn't have me and the Air Corps would. So I decided to go ahead and be a hero in the air. Before they called me to learn how to fly, I practiced in a chair. I put my feet on imaginary rudders and when I wanted to go right I pushed left and when I wanted to go left I pushed right and I could foresee no problem.

The problem I failed to foresee was that flight instructors have little patience with a student who insists that a left rudder will make an airplane turn right. I couldn't get that out of my head. I could for a while but when I was confronted with a stress situation, such as landing the airplane on the ground, I would revert to Ammerman Street and stomp the wrong pedal.

We were flying two-winged Stearmans, which enjoy doing ground loops. I never did solo. This was fortunate for me and the Air Corps as well. Because I would have destroyed the airplane and probably killed myself.

I asked them to send me to bombardier school. They sent me instead to a replacement camp at Scott Field, Illinois. This was a dreadful place.

Every other day, we did kitchen police duty. They got us up at three in the morning and we scrubbed pots and pans until nine o'clock at night. Alternate days were easy. They didn't get us up until six and we spent the day pushing GI brooms through the asphalt streets of Scott Field.

I was in that place for about six weeks, and they were the worst weeks of my life. It was like being in a concentration camp. The winter was bitter and the tar-paper barracks were heated with coal. The coal stoves gave off an awful soot which settled on the snow and made it gray. Gray snow.

The guys in my barracks were all washouts and goof-offs and failures. Each of us had been given a chance for achievement in the Army and had come up short. Now we'd been put away in this low-grade spot, where we could dwell on our shortcomings. The result was that we came up with new shortcomings. We even quit shaving and bathing and nobody cared. We couldn't get passes. We just stayed there and did KP and pushed brooms and felt terrible.

The fellow in the bunk next to mine had a second lieutenant's uniform hanging behind his bunk. He had been almost through pilot training and something really awful happened and he was washed out just ahead of graduation. He had already bought his officer's uniform and his gold bars and his insignia. Now suddenly he was scrubbing pots at Scott Field.

One day when we were on KP I asked him what had happened. He said, "I flew an AT-6 upside down through a hangar." That was a traditional Air Corps answer. It meant, "I don't want to talk about it."

He looked so sloppy in his ill-fitting buck private's GI fatigues. He would sit on his bunk and stare dolefully at that beautiful forest-green officer's jacket. One day a captain came through the barracks and made him get rid of it.

We had some real scoutmasters and Sunday School teachers in that bunch. We had a pharmacist who had washed out of officer candidate school. He kept an assortment of curious pills in his footlocker and sometimes tried to peddle them to us.

We had a guy who came in drunk one night with a barracks bag two-thirds full of whiskey bottles, empty. He had been on scrub duty at the officer's club and had appropriated a bottle and become magnificently sloshed. He had collected those dead soldiers out of the trash.

He did not speak a word. It was late and we were all in our bunks, reading or staring at nothing. He wobbled to the far end of the barracks. Slowly and carefully he took three footlockers and stacked them. Returned to the front where he left his bag. Opened it and brought out an empty, which had held a fifth of scotch. For the next fifteen minutes he bowled those whiskey bottles the length of the barracks and smashed them into the footlockers and they produced a most satisfactory racket.

Not a man in the barracks made a sound. We didn't ask him to stop. We didn't encourage him to continue. We watched him carefully, though. It was the most interesting thing we had seen in weeks, and every one of us understood why he needed to break those bottles.

When he finished he fell on his bunk and slept, with his clothes on. The next morning a dozen or more men were up early with GI brooms, to sweep up the little sea of shattered glass. The bowler did not help us.

I was put into radio school, and life improved. At least on weekends I got to go into Saint Louis and find places where girls and music were. One night in a bar I talked to what we then called an older woman. I liked her face and she had once lived in Fort Worth. She knew where George Clarke Elementary was. I went home with her and she scrambled eggs and I slept on her sofa.

The next weekend I slept in her bed. It was an education. She did all the marvelous things I had done with the prettiest girls in school, but only in my fantasies. She did them for real. She was about thirty-two. A beautiful age for a woman. She was fat in some places and flat in others and she had a sort of cackling laugh that annoyed me, but not enough that I kept away.

Every weekend I would call her. Sometimes she would tell me not to come. The last time I went I was flat broke, not a rare condition for a buck private making fifty bucks a month. I thumbed a ride into town. I didn't even have a nickel to phone her. But I could ride free on the streetcar. During that war, when a person in uniform got on a streetcar in Saint Louis, the motorman put his hand over the coin box. I rode to within about three blocks of her house and punched the bell and a buck sergeant came to the door. I swear he looked like a professional wrestler.

He asked, "Whatta *you* want?"

I told him I had the wrong house and hurried off. After that I was afraid to go back. Margie. Her name was Margie.

Morse code was easy for me and I got along all right in radio school. Just before I graduated I was offered a shot at officer candidate school, to become a communications officer.

I turned it down because I wanted in the war. I would get letters from Bodie and he would be on a PBY or something wonderful like that and he'd be riding along the coast looking for enemy submarines to bomb. Dude would be in the Marshall Islands, or the Solomons, or somewhere just as good. If the war ended, I would go home and all I'd be able to say was that I'd learned to copy Morse code at twenty-five words per minute and dismantle a .50-caliber machine gun blindfolded. Fat lot of heroics.

I thought I already knew what a communications officer did. Not a damn thing but ride herd on a bunch of radio operators and vacuum-tube testers. I couldn't think of a chapter in all of military history where a communications officer was a hero.

They sent me to Arizona to aerial gunnery school. That's where I learned to dismantle the machine gun. Gunnery school was a little more to my taste. I couldn't fly an airplane but I supposed I could ride on one and shoot down enemy planes and return home unashamed.

I had read a good deal about the war in Europe and decided that I wanted to be on a B-17 in the Eighth Air Force, which was based in England. The B-17 outfits flew across the English Channel and bombed Berlin and their aerial gunners got a lot of glory in the papers and the newsreels. That's what I wanted—the B-17, the Eighth Air Force, and England.

Therefore they put me on a B-24 and sent me to the Fifteenth Air Force in Italy.

I had never been within a mile of a B-24. In gunnery school we had flown in B-17s and we decided they were the only decent bombers. We heard nothing but bad news about B-24s. They were death traps. They had too much fuselage and not enough wing surface. They couldn't fly at high altitudes to escape enemy flak. Whatever you do, we said, never, never fly on a B-24.

So there I was, on a B-24. We called it the Four-Engined Whore.

At Lincoln, Nebraska, I was assigned to a crew, four officers and six enlisted men. Our copilot, Lieutenant Block, had never been any closer to a B-24 than I had. He had trained as a medium bomber pilot and now he was about to go overseas and fight the war in an airplane he had never flown.

Our pilot was Lieutenant Ondracka out of Chicago. He managed to convince us that the B-24 would really fly. The other officers besides Block were Hasty, navigator, and Boeckle, bombardier. They were all lieutenants. The enlisted men were all sergeants. Maxwell, engineer. Plumlee, nose gunner. Irwin, ball turret gunner. Scatena, waist gunner. Lamb, tail gunner. I was radio operator and top turret gunner. We would all be together, day and night, on the ground and in the air, for a year and a half.

We flew practice missions several weeks up in Idaho at Mountain Home and then went on to Italy. We had hoped to fly over but we didn't get to. It was traditional that bomber crews were issued their own airplane, so they could name it and paint it and personalize it and fly it across the ocean and fight the war in it. Just about the time we thought we were going to get our bomber, that tradition died.

We crossed the Atlantic in the belly of a Liberty ship. Twenty-nine days of pitching and wallowing, from Newport News, Virginia, to Bari, Italy, on the Adriatic.

We had not heard very much about what B-24 outfits had done from Italy, except for the low-level bombing raids on the Ploesti Oil Fields of Rumania. That was all over by the time we got there. The tough targets for the heavy bombers in Italy had become Vienna and Munich. B-24s didn't go to Berlin from Italy. Too far.

We moved into tents on a base at Lecce, in the heel of the

Italian boot. We thought we'd get our airplane at last but we were disappointed again. No crew flew the same bomber all the time. We didn't know what plane we would get for a mission until about an hour before we took off.

Anyhow, we were there, in Europe, where the war was, and we were eager to get going. And our first assignment was: all-night guard duty. There had been a lot of thievery going on. I am not talking about the enemy. I am talking about our own guys, American GIs, stealing stuff off our bombers. Draining gas. Lifting radios and instruments. Anything that could be converted into cash on the black market. We were issued .45 pistols and assigned a B-24 to stay on all night and guard.

Italians out of Lecce and smaller towns nearby simply could not be kept off that base. They would filter in at night and steal or beg for food, for clothing, for anything. My first night on guard duty a ground crew member told me about an Italian woman who had sneaked aboard a bomber about a week before. She was evidently after food. Boxes of K-rations were kept on the planes in survival kits, in case of bailouts or crashes in enemy territory. This woman had been trapped on board the plane when the ground crew arrived, about 4 A.M., to warm up the engines. She leaped out on the hardstand and ran into a propeller. The ground crew fellow wanted me to go look, right over there, at the dried blood and stuff that was still on the tarmac.

This was not the kind of war I was expecting.

Our crew didn't fly together our first mission. We were divided up and went with other crews made up of strangers. Lieutenant Ondracka and I were assigned to the same airplane. He would sit in as copilot for a Captain Thurmond. I doubt he had sat in the copilot's seat of a B-24 since early in his training. I would ride along as a waist gunner. I hadn't fired a gun from the waist of a bomber since gunnery school in Arizona and from a B-24, never. So we would go into combat under strange conditions.

The night before our first trip, I lay in my bunk late and

listened to the pitchings and rustlings and throat-clearings of Maxwell and Irwin and Plumlee and Scatena and Lamb. They weren't sleeping, either.

This is what I had been hankering for, to be in the war. I confess I wasn't as eager as I had planned to be. That business about the Italian woman running into the prop, that had got to me. The main thing about it was the way the ground crew man had described it. Casually, as if some kind of wild animal had run into the propeller and got its parts scattered. I mean it didn't seem right, or fair. War was supposed to be honorable. I had read that somewhere.

Next morning after briefing, I stood with Lieutenant Ondracka on the pad by the airplane. I was reminded of Dude and me, and how we would be embarrassed by our own feelings. Ondracka was putting up an admirable front. He was about twenty-eight then, a strapping wide-shouldered heavynecked football player type. I felt for him. He was a leader and had to behave like one. I could stand back, and be ordinary, and sink into the doubts about myself. This was a comfort that Ondracka couldn't afford. When the Jeep brought Thurmond and his officers, Ondracka jerked a thumb at me, and then at his chest. He said, "Well, Captain, you're going to get a couple of cherries today."

The target was Munich.

What you hoped for on your first mission was a nice bridge up in northern Italy, where the antiaircraft guns numbered about a dozen. Munich was another matter. The Germans had hundreds of guns there.

On the way across the Adriatic there was nothing much to do. Now and then the pilot would come on the intercom and tell us to keep sharp, watch out for fighters. But German fighters didn't often come out to challenge bombers crossing into southern Europe. At least not this late in the war. They laid back and waited until after the planes had made their bomb runs and turned around. Maybe then there would be a cripple, a bomber with an engine out, or two engines, and it would be unable to keep up with the other planes. It would drop out of formation and become a straggler and that's when the fighters were most likely to strike.

Being shot at for the first time is a great weirdness.

On the bomb run the sky was speckled with black puffs of antiaircraft bursts, all around us. I didn't want to look out at them but how could I not look out? I would miss the war if I didn't. The bursts came in pretty deadly flower patterns, unfurling, then curling at the top. The close ones you could hear. *Thunk. Thoob.* When you could hear a 105 millimeter shell bursting, it usually meant you would at least get flak holes in the airplane. You could see the holes appear. Most of them small, less than two inches in diameter. One of our jobs in the waist was to watch what the shrapnel hit when it passed through. Be sure it didn't clip a control cable, or fray one, or go through an oxygen tank. We were supposed to watch the engines and wings for gas or oil leaks that flak might have caused. I had a hard time keeping my mind on such things.

I couldn't quit thinking about the boy we had heard about at briefing. He was nineteen. He wasn't in our squadron. He had been on his first mission the day before, flying with a strange crew just as Lieutenant Ondracka and I were, and he had caught a chunk of flak in a bad place. The men talked about how rotten it was he was killed on his first mission, just as if it wouldn't be rotten if he had been killed on his tenth or his thirty-second. I did not know that boy but I thought about him when we were passing four miles high over Munich on my own first mission.

It wasn't the way I thought it would be. I thought the action would be wild and frantic and fast. To me it was slow. The flak bursts unfurled in slow motion. The bombardier and the pilot spoke to one another on the intercom in a draggy drawl. The bombers I could see from my window were almost not moving. They seemed held back, suspended. When bombs fell from their bays, the bombs descended softly and slowly.

When I was a young kid and would get sick and have a high fever, the movement of things around me would be slow in that same way. Sounds and scenes would be distant and unreal. Riding over Munich was like that. People down there were shooting at us and trying to kill us but it wasn't real, it wasn't actually happening.

When we got back out over the Adriatic on the way home and I had caught no chunk of flak in a bad place, I began to get silly. A common reaction. First-mission sillies. Some guys laughed. Some cried. Some sang and told bad jokes. I sensed an extraordinary relief, and yet I felt high, and floating. I had not done a damn thing, but I seemed to have achieved something extraordinary. I had simply ridden along in an airplane that was being shot at by a lot of Germans, and they missed. I had not made a contribution of any kind. I hadn't even seen an enemy fighter. The only thing I'd done was lose my cherry.

When our crew began flying together, all of us slept better the night before a mission. I rode in the top turret above the flight deck, just behind the cockpit, where I had trained to ride.

The summer of '44 we weren't losing a lot of crew lives but now and then a guy would catch a piece of flak, like the young man on his first mission, and sometimes an entire crew would be lost.

Vienna was considered our toughest target and before I was through I went there six times. On one of those trips I was looking ahead, at a group of B-24s creeping over the target, and one of the airplanes just exploded. Blooey, and it was gone, and ten guys with it. A direct hit in the belly. Pieces of airplane went twisting down. Parts of wings, tail section, engines. When you saw that, it made an impression, especially when the airplane you were on was following the one that got hit, and the gunners who hit it were still shooting.

When we talked about getting hit, we talked in jokes. We talked about minor wounds. Little piece of flak, say, in the thigh, or the calf. Even the shoulder wouldn't be bad. Get you a Purple Heart and a couple of weeks in the hospital. Most guys said where they didn't want to get hit was in the head.

Funny thing, getting hit in the head wasn't such a terrible idea to me. Maybe because I had gotten so many licks there already. Sometimes I felt that the bony protrusions on my skull were a protection, a thickness that the others didn't have. My greatest fear was getting hit in the balls. I had nightmares about catching a chunk of flak there.

On bomb runs we wore protective flak suits, which were bulky versions of bullet-proof vests that draped across the shoulders. Then we had flak helmets, heavy things that came down over the ears. All that was fine but none of it protected my family jewels.

About our fifth or sixth mission I couldn't stand it any longer. I went to the armorers' shop and told them about my problem. They laughed but they took an old flak suit and cut me a special rig. When we were in heavy flak zones I shoved it under me and sat on it. The front of it tapered so I could pull it up onto my lower belly and tie it. A sort of jock strap. After that I felt more secure. I took a lot of hell about my flak-proof jock strap but I didn't care. I wore it. As far as I know, it was the only such device in the European Theater of Operations.

Heavy-bomber crews like ours in the Fifteenth Air Force at the time we were flying were required to complete fifty missions as a tour. Then we could go home. We began seeing ourselves as existing in percentages of fifty. When we had ten missions, we were twenty-percent alive. At twenty-five missions we were fifty-percent alive. And so on to fifty, when at last we wouldn't have to go out again and would be survivors, a hundred-percent alive.

When we went out to the airplane for our twentieth trip, a lieutenant and a buck sergeant were standing beneath the wing, looking embarrassed. They were from a new crew, assigned to fly with us on their first mission. Not many weeks before, Ondracka and I had looked that same way. Now suddenly we were considered veterans, qualified to be shepherds of timid guys going out for the first time.

That gave me confidence, and I began to feel the old itch to be a hero. Our first few missions I had lost that itch. I was too busy concentrating on staying alive. Now I reminded myself that I would never again, no matter how old I became, have a better chance to be a hero.

Our target was Vienna and its marshalling yards. On the bomb run we had got into a mess. We had lost an engine and Ondracka got hit. When bombs were away and we peeled off the target, Maxwell jerked on my boot, our signal that he needed me on the flight deck. I came down and saw Ondracka's head was not straight. It was fallen to one side. I jerked at his oxygen mask and it was full of blood. We almost never pulled him out of his seat. He seemed to weigh a ton and a half. We got him down on the deck and I cut away his flight jacket where the chunk of flak had gone in. A big hole in his ribs. I shook an entire packet of sulfa powder on the wound and got a compress on it and waited to see if the bleeding stopped and if his emergency oxygen was flowing all right. He was still unconscious but his color wasn't bad. I didn't know the fighters had jumped us until two slugs zipped through the plexiglass dome of my upper turret—right where my head would have been if I hadn't come down to the flight deck. I got back in my seat in time to see two Messerschmitts starting their pursuit curve from eight o'clock high. I framed the lead plane in my sight and tracked him until I couldn't miss and put two long bursts into him and he exploded. That made six kills for me. No, wait, seven, because I'd gotten one the day before. Lamb the tail gunner was yelling on the intercom, "Six o'clock level! I'm jammed! I can't fire! I can't fire!" This was more like the combat I had dreamed of, and seen in movies. Fast, loud, and wild. A fighter coming in level on your tail is the easiest shot in the sky. I kept the triggers down on those twin-mounted .50-calibers for a lot longer burst than the book recommended. I watched tracer after tracer go into the Messerschmitt's prop and I think one slug must have got the pilot because he just kept coming. I swear to God I thought he would fly up our tailpipe, but at the last second he sailed beneath us, and Irwin in the belly turret and Plumlee in the nose watched him fly into a mountain. That made eight for me. I felt a stickiness in the arm of my jacket. I got a glove off and ran my hand inside the jacket to my upper arm and brought out blood, so I'd been popped. It didn't hurt much. I decided to let it go for the time being because Maxwell was jerking at my boot again. The airplane was weaving and I supposed that Block the copilot was flying evasive action. "I think he's sick or something," Maxwell said. I pulled his goggles up and looked at Block's eyes. Sick, hell, he'd been hit. While I watched, his eyes disappeared up in his head and we had what you call a Situation—a B-24 at 20,000 feet without a pilot. The airplane slipped off to the left and lost a thousand feet of altitude before I fell into Ondracka's seat and got it straightened out. Maxwell's face was grave. I told him, "Somebody's got to fly this thing home, and land it." He said quickly, "You fly it. You're the aviation cadet." He could pick the worst times to be funny. Aviation cadet, yeah, one who never soloed because he couldn't land a primary trainer. But I didn't get any volunteers to take my seat. It was a long, long ride home. Fortunately there wasn't much banking to do, and the tower cleared the area and let us come in straight off the Adriatic without even flying the landing pattern. Maxwell helped with the throttles and called out the air speed and we got the airplane down without doing it much more damage than it already had. I kicked the wrong rudder only once, which was enough to put one wheel off the runway and we ended up with the nose stuck into a grove of olive trees. Maxwell switched off the engines. I didn't even know how to do it. A pain in my arm and I thought, "That's my Purple Heart hurting." Pretty soon the medics were on the flight deck, working with the pilots, and one of them said, "Cry sake, Mac, lookit who landed this sumbitch. A fuckin' radio operator." A month later I stood at attention on the parade ground and a general read from a piece of paper and awarded me the Distinguished Flying Cross and the Purple Heart. I thought about how the ribbons would line up on my chest. Look all right: the DFC, the Purple Heart, the Air Medal with clusters, and the European Theater of Operations. I would wear them when I went back to Eastland and sat on the front stool at the Corner Drug soda fountain. I would stare into the street with solemn eyes, and try to pretend I didn't want to talk about it all.

The fact is, I really didn't want to talk about it when I got home. At least I didn't want to tell the truth.

For several years I wasn't able to admit that I flew fifty combat missions over southern Europe without once firing a shot at an enemy plane, or getting as much as a skinned finger in the way of wounds. When I was finally able to make that admission, I began working on a more difficult one. Which was, that my entire military career was of no consequence whatever.

I am not referring to our country's participation in that great war, which cost so many precious lives. I am talking about my personal part in it. The hard truth is that if I had stayed home and operated a rivet gun in an airplane plant, I would have made a greater contribution. I am not certain I even saw an enemy plane. Once I thought I did and swung my guns around to line it up in my sight. But then somebody said it was a P-51, which was one of our own planes that from some angles resembled a Messerschmitt 109.

All those months I spent training as a combat radio operator? I did less radio operating in the war than I did gunnery. After we got to Italy I did not send or receive one message. B-24s out of Italy flew in groups of several squadrons and only the lead bomber, one airplane, had a radio operator who did any operating. The others of us simply rode along, and spent a lot of our time listening to Axis Sally play Glenn Miller records out of Berlin.

I flew my last mission early in 1945. The tradition in our squadron was that when a crew member got home from any mission, he went to Medics and got a free shot of whiskey, a double, and it was good stuff. I mean it was American bourbon, the worst of which was far better than the awful stuff available in Italy.

The whiskey tradition was refined when a guy flew his last mission. On that occasion the entire crew—all the enlisted men, in my case—went with him to the medical office and he got not only his personal shot of whiskey but theirs as well. He had to drink it in the presence of a medic, though. Quite a lot of booze. Six doubles. You see why they wanted a medic present.

I was into the fourth shot when I noted a figure beneath a white sheet in the examining room. I asked who it was. "Show you," the medic said, and pulled the sheet back. It was a body of a crewman, still in his flight suit, and half his face was gone. I went outside and vomited and didn't want what was left of my whiskey.

The worst mistake I made in military service was coming home as soon as I finished my missions.

They said to me, "All right, you've flown your tour but you don't have to go home if you're not ready. You can type and we can use you here, on a desk job. You can stay on combat status which means you'll get your flight pay as well as your base pay but you'll never have to fly another mission."

I didn't want to stay at Lecce but I could have gone somewhere else. To Naples. Rome. Occupied Germany. France. England. I had no reason to rush home. Nobody was depending on me there. I wasn't even in love at the time, or at least not very deep. The Army was offering me the chance to experience, expenses paid, a great part of the world, and I didn't have sense enough to take it.

"Send me home," I said. And they did.

On May 7, 1945, when the Germans quit, I was on the *S.S. Mariposa* in the middle of the Atlantic. That vessel was bringing home hundreds of wounded men. Men with one leg. Or with no legs. Men who couldn't use crutches because they had no arms. Men wrapped head to toe in bandages. I walked among them and saw their pain, and felt it, and I was ashamed that I had ever wished for a cheap Purple Heart so I could feel a hero. A whistle blew and a voice on the ship's loudspeaker announced the German surrender. The war in Europe was over. I was on the deck where the wounded men were when the announcement came. There was no rejoicing.

The following autumn when the Japanese had surrendered and fighting everywhere stopped, I was working on an Army newspaper at Santa Monica. On November 4 they set me free. I had my mustering-out pay in my pocket, a wad of bills almost as big as the one Uncle Barney won in San Angelo that time. I felt absolutely rich. I went to Los Angeles and sat in the nicest bar I could find. I had learned to like bars. I met a fellow and his wife who were about to drive nonstop all the way to Fort Worth. They said I could ride along as far as Abilene if I'd kick in thirty-five dollars to help buy gas. I peeled off three tens and a five and pitched them on the bar. Spending money was fun when you had a lot of it.

That night, while we hummed across Arizona, I sat in the back seat and grinned into the darkness. I felt fine about my future. The hell with being a hero. I had come through a tour of combat without any scars and I didn't have to be entirely candid about not shooting at anybody. I would let everybody assume that a guy with fifty missions under his belt just didn't care to talk about the painful details.

I could see my 2,400 dollar bills, waiting for me in the bank at home. They were in several stacks, neat and crisp and beautiful. They would be enough to get me through my last semester at school, buy a car and some civilian clothes, and finance a big homecoming party with all my friends. I was determined to have that party, even if it cost me a couple of hundred bucks.

Epilogue

ABOUT THIRTY-FIVE YEARS after I discovered in those mirrors that I was a funny-looking kid, my bone disease was diagnosed as polyostotic fibrous dysplasia.

Doctors call this disease a "developmental disorder," which means they don't really know its cause. Apparently the trouble goes back to some unhappy accident in the development of the fetus. Whatever that accident might be has not been determined.

Fibrous dysplasia somehow destroys healthy bone and replaces it with a bonelike fibrous tissue. Bony lesions form, often in places where the victim receives a sharp blow, as when I got the lick above the eye with that rock in Fort Worth. A variety of deformities may occur over a large part of the skeleton. Asymmetry of the face and skull is common, as in my own case, and some victims have severe pain. If any drug has been effective in the treatment of this disease, I have not been told about it.

I count myself lucky because, while fully half my skeleton is affected, I have not been incapacitated by the disease. I've always been able to function, at least physically. Emotionally, the disorder has been the predominant influence in my life. In the work I do, avoiding audiences and mirrors has not been easy, but I admit I have given it the old university try.

In recent years, when I have felt more at peace with myself,

I have been able to see that in one sense this disorder has had a positive effect. I have received considerable recognition, in Texas at least, as a professional writer. Many Texans get a little too enthusiastic about themselves when they receive favorable notice, and my physical abnormality has surely kept me from that. One thing certain: Nobody carrying the lumps and bumps of fibrous dysplasia on his face and skull is going to become an egotist, not as long as mirrors are around.

Every five years at Eastland we have a community homecoming. Anyone who ever attended our high school or lived in our town is invited. At the last homecoming a big fellow came grinning up to me and it was Dude, returned from traveling over half the planet on his engineering job.

He said, "How about let's get up early in the morning and go squirrel hunting?"

It seemed a good homecoming sort of thing to do so we went. I didn't tell Dude that I had long ago quit killing things. I picked a big pecan tree and said I would sit there and still-hunt. He nodded and went on down the creek. I sat and watched dawn come, and sunrise. I watched a couple of young squirrels playing tag in the pecan. I didn't load the gun I had. It was Dude's, the same little .22 target rifle I borrowed the day I fell on the rocks, out south of town, and the gun had fired and the slug came so near hitting me in the head. That was getting close to fifty years ago. All that time had been given to me, by a near miss.

When the sun got up, Dude came back and sat beside me. He said, "Do you remember what we left in the crack of the rock on Deep Creek in 1938?"

The two coins. The buffalo nickels.

"I wonder if we could find them," he said. "When we hid them we said we'd come back sometime, and look."

We laughed a little about the idea—two old guys with graying hair, driving thirty miles to look for ten cents they'd hidden in a rock when they were boys. But we went.

I asked Dude if he understood, when we left the coins,

what they represented and he said, "I don't guess I did. But I've always known they were important, and that some day we'd come back and try to find them."

On the way we talked about our times on the river, and the roaming we did, and the old car we never built.

Dude knew exactly where to leave the highway and stop and go through the fence. We walked half a mile into the mesquite and found the place with no trouble. One of the trees we'd used to mark the spot had died, and the ledge had sloughed off and the coins were buried. We couldn't find them. On the way home we talked of other things.

In 1958 my mother died of cancer, the only illness of any consequence she had in her seventy years. Her death was a surprise to us. We had long been prepared for our father to go first. He'd had a couple of heart attacks and a stroke and our mother had cared for him as if he might drop off at any hour.

He had retired from the store in Abilene and they had moved back to Eastland, into another rented house. I can count thirty-six houses my mother lived in during her marriage, and she left every one of them cleaner and in better condition than she found it.

I did not cry at her funeral. I wasn't able to.

A few weeks after we buried her my sisters and I went through her possessions. We found boxes and sacks and bags of things she had quietly collected, but had no room for in the small houses and apartments they rented. These were meant to replace a part of what she lost in the warehouse in Fort Worth, and she intended to use them in the house of her own she hoped to get. She didn't get it, but she never stopped hoping.

We found one item that struck me as especially symbolic of her life. For years and years she saved the small cotton drawstring tobacco sacks that my father emptied. She ripped out the seams and washed and ironed the sacks and stitched them together to make the backing for a full-sized quilt. She didn't need scrap material that desperately but the tobacco sacks appealed to her—rescuing cloth that would have become waste from a bad habit, and making of it something useful and good.

When we found the quilt with the tobacco-sack backing, then I cried.

My father died four years later. I believe he lived that time in a state of wonder, that he had outlived his wife. He must also have been in a state of frustration. He was free of responsibility and could roam across the country the way he'd always dreamed. But his health wouldn't let him go.

He never lost the itch in his foot. Up to the end he loved roads, and the way they looked between towns. When I was in the Army he traced me on maps through Oklahoma, Kansas, Nebraska, Arizona, California, Kentucky, Idaho. He would want to know about the highways, the bridges, the stops along the way.

Shortly before he died I visited him in Eastland. When I entered his room in the hospital he was looking at an old map of Europe that he'd used to track me when I was overseas during the war. He put a shaky finger on Italy and said, "Tell me how the road looks between Salerno and Naples."

A long time after I had quit yearning to become a hero, I became one, and in a most unexpected way.

My children were ten and twelve. They were growing up as city kids. One Sunday I took them with me to the farm of a friend so they could get a look at country life. We stayed late, until milking time, and as a joke my friend asked if I'd like to milk one of his cows. I said, also as a joke, that I'd be happy to.

All the angels in heaven knew I could milk a cow, but my own children did not. They were surprised. More than that. They were dumbfounded, overwhelmed. When the first streams of milk hit the bottom of my bucket, those children whooped. They laughed. They ran about in circles and leaped in the air. Their father, milking a cow. It was a miracle.

They had never seemed impressed by what I did for a liv-

ing. I didn't even go to an office in the morning the way normal fathers did. I stayed home and tapped on a typewriter.
Like a secretary.

But milking, that was something else. I don't believe I ever
did anything, before or after, that thrilled them more. They
went around the neighborhood talking about their father, the
hero, who could milk a cow.

PAPER HERO
has been set in Bembo type by
G&S TYPESETTERS
printed by HART GRAPHICS
bound by ELLIS BINDERY
designed by
WHITEHEAD & WHITEHEAD
1986